I RE

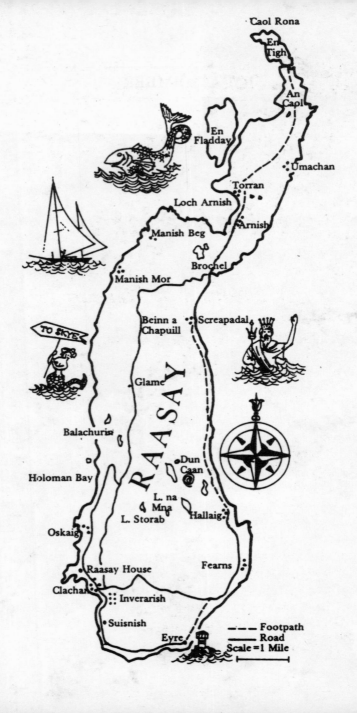

JOHN NICOLSON

I Remember

Memories of Raasay

Birlinn

This edition first published in 2002 by
Birlinn Limited
West Newington House
10 Newington Road
Edinburgh
EH9 1QS

www.birlinn.co.uk

First published in 1989 by
The Pentland Press, Edinburgh

ISBN 1 84158 222 0

British Library Cataloguing-in-Publication Data
A catalogue record for this book is available
from the British Library

Typeset by Edderston Book Design, Peebles
Printed and bound by Cox & Wyman Ltd, Reading

To Catriona

AUTHOR'S NOTE

This book owes much to the help of friends.

My special thanks go to Donald Daltrey, Joyce Steadman and Tony Hunter for much valued advice, to Alexander and Margaret Moodie for photographs, to John Macleod (East Molesey) for sketches, to Derek Cooper, Fred Macaulay and Roddy Kennedy for their constructive criticism and helpful suggestions, to Dr John MacInnes and members and friends of the Gaelic Society of London for their encouragement, and to the publishers for their kind consideration.

CONTENTS

FOREWORD

John Nicolson calls this book his 'story and his song'. It has, indeed, elements of both, and both are fascinating. The story tells of a boyhood and adolescence set in the twenties and thirties, in the idyllic surroundings of the Island of Raasay, lying between Skye and the north-western mainland of Scotland. All these communities, island and mainland alike, were then still Gaelic-speaking; English, though well enough known, was largely centred on the school. And there, incredibly, children who had never even seen a bus, let alone a train, had to memorise such things as the names of railway stations and the number of spans in the Forth Bridge. That was in Torran, at the north end of Raasay. The crofting townships were linked by footpaths, one of which ran across to the neighbouring tidal island of Fladda, and were substantially self-contained. Work was hard, food was plentiful, and money was scarce.

It is now fifty years ago – and a world away.

Just before the Second World War, the Nicolson family moved to the south end of Raasay, where the amenities of life included metalled roads and connections by steamer with the mainland ports of Kyle of Lochalsh and Mallaig. There was also an hotel: the Taigh-Mór, the Big House, once the home of MacLeod of Raasay and later the residence of clearing landlords whose activities left most of the middle ground of Raasay an uninhabited wilderness. This change of environment from Torran to Oscaig was qualitatively more significant than a move of a few miles within one small island community might suggest. We see it here through the eyes of a sensitive 14-year-old boy, and the impressions that he registers are instructive. Throughout the whole book, it is that same perceptiveness, sharpening the asides of his vivid conversational style, that gives the recital of events the lyrical quality that the author calls 'song'.

In so many ways it is a celebratory song; most of all a celebration of the crofting community of the north end in his boyhood days.

Here was a society that practised the exchange of gifts: 'There was a wonderful community spirit. When we had no potatoes or milk, neighbours supplied some . . . When we had milk . . . we returned the compliment. The teacher, who had no croft, was well looked after and there was no question of money changing hands, but she reciprocated in her own way . . . A bartering system without any question of being as a repayment did wonders for goodwill'.

For all that, there is no sentimentalising, no false reverence, no suggestion of a seamless society or a tensionless Golden Age. John writes as a member of a community in which individuals – and what resolute individuals these men and women were – are allowed their virtues, their foibles, their quirks of personality. He is realistic, often playful, but he is never demeaning. These are his kinsfolk and his own people.

His harshest criticisms are directed at religious life. Wherever in Christendom the faith is an integral part of society, there, too, is a parallel, anti-clerical tradition; and this is a local example. The great 'Apostle of the North' said much the same in his own time with regard to hypocritical vapourings and false gloom. But after John's strictures, some of which are pretty severe, the impact of the following passage is all the more powerful: 'Churchgoers who were true believers . . . followed a way of life that had no discernible blemish. They were kindly, courteous and sincere. They had time for us young people who were around them and by deeds and words showed concern for our material and spiritual welfare . . . I was privileged to have enjoyed their company during the formative years of my life and I cherish their memory . . . penniless as they so often were but richly endowed with spiritual blessings . . .'.

It is only in the margins of this tale, so to speak, that the reader will sense the sheer incomparable beauty of the island of Raasay. That, too, endorses the authenticity of his account. In Raasay, as no doubt others did elsewhere, we accepted the landscape as a part of the natural order. But there was a constant awareness of the dominating presence of the sea. The qualities of versatility and self-reliance that the islanders needed to develop for their very survival, particularly before the advent of fast, modern communications, are exemplified in John Nicolson's own subsequent life as a mariner. This first part of his autobiography takes us into the early 1940s and the beginnings of a brilliant career in the service of the merchant navy. That, as he himself would say, is another story. I hope we shall all be able to read it before long.

February, 1989   John MacInnes
                                   University of Edinburgh

INTRODUCTION

The narrative, other than passing references to later years, spans the first part of my life into my twentieth year. Detailed information about Raasay's island history, rock formation, flora and fauna may be obtained from other books, compiled by writers well versed in their subjects. I have tried to convey my own impressions of a way of life in an island community.

Some may feel that parts of these impressions could have been left unsaid. When it became known that I was making jottings, the message was conveyed to me, in a friendly but forcible way, that I owed much to church influence in my formative years. I do not know what it was presumed or anticipated that I would be writing about the church but I saw 'Church Influence' as the kind of chapter heading for which I was searching. Parental and school influences were not mentioned by my 'mentors' and I have since wondered why it had been suggested to me that I should avoid references to the church – in which indeed I had been baptised.

In allowing myself some literary licence, various incidents are recalled without the benefit of a diary, but simply from memory. As I stood recently looking at the ruins of my uncle's thatched home in Torran on a warm summer's day, memories flooded in of near relations and neighbours who had enriched my childhood; of the sitings of the barn, the byre, the well and the patches where children played – now all overgrown with birch trees, ling and rushes.

The house where I was born these many years ago has since been given a face-lift, but more memories than I have referred to remain with me – some too personal and 'in family' for general interest. Our childhood play-places both at the back of the house and near the schoolhouse are also overgrown. All that seems to have continuity is the brook at the end of the house, a mere rill in the summer season – but never drying up – and letting the passer-by know:

> For some may come and some may go
> But I go on forever.

As I reminisced in the midday sun, so close to nature, surveying the peaceful scene:

> I lay my head upon a pillow –
> A pillow of contentment by a stream
> Meandering through a vale of visions,
> Enchanted held by many versions of a dream.
>
> A thousand memories danced in a ripple
> Each one impressed upon the scroll of mind.
> Realities of life were dreams – and dreams were real,
> Cradled in codicils and afterthoughts refined.

I reflected on the 'Four Freedoms' made famous by Franklin D. Roosevelt – 'freedom of speech; freedom of worship; freedom from want; and freedom from fear'. They were all here in the solitude and tranquillity of Torran, but who was there to deny them? Such is the irony of life.

Some traditions embracing religion, language, literature and music are well worth preserving as part of the Highland heritage. Other traditions, such as over-emphasis on religion through sectarianism, and the use of alcohol, do not fall into that category, but they live on. Gaels are often over-sensitive about their upbringing, and there is no good reason for this being the case. The younger generation, who enjoy a more agreeable life-style, are less introverted, and that is all to the good.

I recall in the early sixties meeting considerable opposition from Hebridean colleagues when it was proposed by

Jimmy Paterson, of Greenock stock, and Murdo Macdonald, from Breakish in Skye, that the Gaelic Society of London should, as part of the Annual Highland Gathering in London, create a reproduction of a crofter's cottage. There was in evidence the bristling of a defence mechanism to prevent any ridicule of a past way of life.

The proposition was carried; but talk about 'making rods for our own backs'! Jimmy, Murdo and I were left to find nets, lobster-pots and creels, and to transport them with other bric-a-brac, such as oil lamps and ewers, as best we could, to Clapham Common where the gathering was held. Two Uist lassies, Christine Laing and Marion Macleod, rummaged through the warehouses in Richmond, Surrey, and our thatched 'wee hoose', with considerable help from Sir Robert Macalpine's organisation, exhibited various items which brought a lump to the throat of more than one older visitor. Those on the committee who had not favoured the project were agreeably surprised at its success, due to the interest that was generated. The Glasgow Lewis and Harris Association, in enacting comedy sketches, get very close to the mark when depicting an island way of life. Perhaps life is too short to be taken too seriously! The package of life, unfortunately, also offers sorrow, and where better is sadness depicted and reflected than in the traditional Gaelic songs which have world-wide appeal?

Future generations will wish to know how their predecessors lived. History books, as was the case in my own school-days, can be one-sided or incomplete. It is in this context that it is important to keep traditions alive and preserve the language, literature and music of Gaeldom. On analysis, it might be concluded that the projection of culture and traditions, by practical and reasonable means, should find favour, even if on occasion the considerations are secondary and may even be a means to an end.

I am quite sure there are abler pens than mine that could

write about and itemise the components of a Hebridean island home. This, however, is my song and my story! It is from the heart and I can only hope that readers, some of whom may identify themselves with sentiments that have been expressed, may find some solace and a little pleasure in these reflections. Others, few and forgiving I trust, who may not be so favourably disposed, 'need not wear the hat unless it fits'. I ask them to gloss over my weaknesses and remember me in their prayers.

'There is perhaps nothing an educated man or woman can do which requires less intelligence than the writing of books' – Hilaire Belloc.

CHAPTER 1

THE OPENING YEARS

Of beauty rare in quiet seas
Lies Raasay in the Hebrides;
A jewel set among the Isles
Enchanted held by nature's smiles.

Thus I enthused at the ripe age of fifteen with schooldays one year behind me. Metre and rhythm – what did they matter, as my feet scattered wild bluebells in the woods above Oscaig and I retrieved yet another fuel piece of silver tree, or was it spruce? The environment was all around me and environmentalists had not been heard of in such rural settings. There were plenty more bluebells where these came from and surely there was plenty of wood all around as far as the eye could see! It was forbidden to help yourself to logs, even fallen ones if these were larch, in the sacred acres of woodland to which the Forestry Commission laid claim. Logs were used extensively for house fires and a log was a log was a log.

Meantime, the local shoemaker had crunched by in his old Ford car, or was it a Morris? At that time of my life the old man seemed even older than he did twenty-five years later, when, on a crisp spring morning, he, my stepmother and I took a tumble in his car – probably the same one – over the boulders by the seashore in Suishnish. He was also the special constable, the factor, the taxi owner and its driver, the forester, the registrar, the spearhead owner and the man of knowledge, good for a reference and positive in his approach, having fathered a brilliant family of eight. I did not then know about this man's great standing and to me he simply represented the forbidden fruit. I dodged him nimbly and was soon back home with as much wood as I could carry on my back, for Uncle Sandy (Trochan) to cut into suitable sized logs to fit the kitchen grate.

Anyway, back to 1925 when I was born in Torran, at the north end of Raasay. I do not remember the event, but I was told recently that I was born prematurely. I do not believe it, even although I seem to have rushed through life ever since. It was on a hot August day that I first saw light. I felt something anyway, and I have a mark on my left thigh to prove it. It was some two weeks after the Portree Communion. These religious festivals were events by which other happenings, births, marriages, deaths, the date when the bull did his duty and the first lifting of potatoes, were identified. The Portree Communion weekend – christened by some unkind wags in Portree as the Raasay Fair, owing to the influx of Raasayites on these twice-yearly occasions – was the signal for the first tasting of home-grown potatoes, usually Kerrs Pinks. It also signified that the bleaching season, which had started in mid-July, was now over. During this period household linen was washed, spread out on hillocks, and allowed to bleach naturally. The process was always successful but we had to watch out for earwigs. Linen shaking was quite a game with youngsters but the fun was soon over if a garment was dropped in the process. The bleaching season would not be back for another year!

Torran means a small heap. Nestling under 'Carn Mor' – the big heap or cairn – and overlooking Loch Arnish, it was at least a pleasant heap of which I have my memories. My predecessors are of Scorrybreac Skye stock, at least on my paternal side, but over the years there was a fair old mixture of Nicolsons, Macswans and Macleods – the last my maternal side – to mention but a few. The Macswans, so the

2

story goes – and who am I to discredit it? – are a sept of the Macleods. In the far distant days, some Macleods were caught thieving of their 'betters'. As they were identifying themselves, one by one, no doubt under threat of death and pressure, one young man, on the point of being interrogated, saw some swans. Knowing that a Macleod had no chance and would be hanged, he answered to the name of Macswan and was set free. Anyway, it is a good story. Like myself, many of my relations are tall, dark and handsome. Indeed, some cousins are distinctly swarthy. A number of Spaniards were washed ashore, alive, after the ill-fated Spanish Armada. When they were fed, watered and warmed up, there was no stopping these hot-blooded fellows, and before long there was more than one young and not so young maiden in the family way. My predecessors came from Rona so no more need be said other than that Highland surnames were at least preserved, which is more than can be said for some of the inhabitants in Barra.

Legend also has it that our family line had the benefit or otherwise of reincarnation. The many crows in Torran were supposed to be long-gone relatives and my Uncle Donald, who was nicknamed 'the Crow', always out of his hearing, would have no-one shoot them unless, perchance, they were caught picking out the eyes of his own sheep or divebombing with unerring accuracy the newly planted potatoes in the drills. In such circumstances he would have shot his own grandmother, and taking belief to its logical conclusion, he probably had a go at his mother-in-law instead! The crow legend lives on with the family, is now quite respectable and the butt of jokes at local weddings. The latest sighting of Mr Corbie has been in Kyle of Lochalsh, and Livingston, where some of Uncle Donald's descendants live.

My earliest recollection of events is of the death of my own mother. She died at the premature age of thirty-eight. I can still see her coffin being passed out through the 'room' window. One other early memory is seeing my aunt, who stepped in to look after us, making a bonfire of bedding and clothing. She was being helped by a neighbour, old cripple Kirsty – and I picked up from their small-talk that these articles had been used by my mother and were much infected. This registered with me and fitted into place later on in my childhood when I was told (quite wrongly) that cancer was grouped with consumption (tuberculosis) as an infectious disease, necessitating the destruction of even the patient's bed. My mother's brass-knobbed iron bed – worth a small fortune nowadays – landed at the bottom of Loch Arnish, probably the last one to do so.

It has at least to be said that in those days, when a little mattered a lot, people had the courage of their convictions and went to extreme lengths to protect the family. The disposal of goods and chattels by fire and brine was an expensive way of life that could be ill-afforded; but what did such material things matter when a family had lost its nearest and dearest? Unfortunately, in the case of tuberculosis, the protection of families came too late and many a young family was wiped out by this scourge up to the third decade of this century. In Raasay, like other parts of the Highlands and Islands of Scotland, interbreeding of the human species did not help. It was not all down to untreated cow's milk.

My father, like all the other locals, was a fisherman, going as far away as Loch Hourn in the herring season. Still, he had been much further in the mercantile marine. We lived in the Mission House in Torran.

I remember, I remember the house where I was born,
The little window where the sun came peeping in at morn.

The Mission House, our home, was attached to the Mission Hall which was known by everyone as 'the church'. It was a well-built house, better than many croft houses, and the expense of building it had been met by the 'Wood' family during their time as landlords. The combined kitchen and living-room next to the church had a high ceiling which did not allow of a room above it. This, one may assume, was to prevent undue noise upstairs upsetting the congregation – and the preacher! There was a small trap-door leading from the stairs' landing to the dark space above the kitchen, where was lodged the family cradle and chattels which, for all I know, may still be there. It was the forbidden part of our home, probably because of the danger of movement cracking the wood lathing between the rafters, which was of course the ceiling of the kitchen below, and injuring life and limb. The 'room' at the other end of the house was where my father and I slept; there was a spare bed reserved for visitors, and no privacy. The wooden partition between the room and the middle room – the closet – was well varnished. Two sets of antlers adorned the partition and on the padded bases rested framed photographs of father and mother in different poses, very Victorian or perhaps Edwardian! The papered back wall against which the beds were placed, end to end, was covered with portraits, mostly of deceased relatives.

Such an arrangement was to be found in every house between Kyle Rona and Brochel Castle. It also happened to be a feature of many Highland croft houses, but I was not to know this at that time. The beds were adorned with white tasselled covers and lace frills which reached the floor. A similar frill, some half metre in depth, ran along the whole length of the wall immediately behind the beds. The 'floor frill' conveniently hid certain receptacles and odds and ends such as spare nets and wool for spinning. An open, highly-glossed blackleaded grate was alcoved under the mantle-piece. A thick velvet pelmet swathed the mantlepiece, on which rested an old wooden-cased clock, various ornaments acquired over the years and yet more family pictures. A rocking-chair and an easy-chair completed the fireside scene. In the corner by the window was a large mahogany chest of drawers which was well used, other than the bottom drawer which was for father's use and sacrosanct. Some memories of mother were treasured among his shirts, stiffly starched collars and 'long johns'.

A large table and six hardwood chairs were by the white lace-curtained window, and near the door to the lobby was a washstand, with ewer, jug and soap-dish. The room was sunny and the window ledge was crammed with geraniums bedded in crocks, and cans which were pasted over with odd bits of wallpaper, frilled at the edge. Further inboard, below one set of the antlers, was a large wooden chest on trestles, fully covered with a white cotton or perhaps linen cloth. On top was a sizeable swivelled mirror on its own stand, the whole doing duty as a dressing table. The wooden floor was covered with waxcloth and three thick home-made rugs, one each in front of the beds and the fireplace. Rug-making provided a pleasant pastime on long wintry nights. Hessian bags were used as a base and strips of discarded garments did duty as rug wool. The rugs lasted for ages and were well designed, sporting a variety of colours. Colour was not a problem as the wallpaper could barely be seen and other software was, in any case, white!

The closet – nothing to do with 'the little room', which did not exist – was also a bedroom and a useful store. The sizeable space above the stairs and the closet were ideal for playing indoor games and also stored personal and household belongings. Milk was kept in covered basins in a space above the stairs, to the front of the house. Here also was a store for jam, about which more later. Also on the stair landing and in the attic bedroom were chests for household linen and personal clothes. Other than overcoats, which, if they were 'Sunday best', were kept on hangers behind room doors (casual coats did not qualify for a hanger), personal clothing including suits, costumes and dresses, was folded carefully and placed in the chests. The chests, to be found in most houses, were well-made, with dovetailed joints. Most had an aperture running along the width of the chest and just below the lid. In it were kept, for the men, folded ties, handkerchiefs, cufflinks, studs and tiepins. For the women, it was a repository for their various adornments and adored fripperies. These smaller chests also had hinged lids and one in our house was cloth-lined and had a lock, which I do not recall ever being used. Perhaps the key was lost!

The kitchen, with its open hearth and fireplace, over which dangled the swee (hook on a chain for kettles, pots and pans), also had a bed. It was a large firm-based iron bed with an inordinate number of brass knobs and rods. It had been supplied by J. D. Williams from Manchester, and judging by its symbols it must have been manufactured for the use of honeymooners. The kitchen was warm and Aunt Mary took full advantage of its comfort even if there was a complete lack of privacy. In this room we all lived. There were two tables, both in use for meals, a long bench by the window, ample hardwood chairs, and one armchair, which Trochan claimed. My sister had a wooden stool with a hole in the middle of the seat which made it easier for Aunt Mary to carry when milking an unresponsive cow. A big dresser with cupboards and drawers, and a double compartment kist for oatmeal and flour, were part of the furnishings. The flour was strong and fresh. Scones and pancakes kept very well for days, whereas nowadays flour products turn stale within hours. The folk of yesteryear would not wish to know about improved nutrient values and additives, other than cream of tartar and baking soda. Even baking powder was not given cupboard room.

A pendulum table clock, now well over one hundred years old and lying in our own house loft, a tea caddy, salt in a tin (to keep it dry), and various bits of brass and knick-knacks covered the mantlepiece, whilst below it and along its whole length was a strong piece of twine which was in continuous use for drying socks. More pictures of people, including King George V and Queen Mary, and at least two calendars, adorned the wall by the fireplace. In a corner below the mantlepiece were also a pincushion and a woollen holder for handling hot pots. Standing on the floor and resting against a pillar of the mantlepiece was a rod (*slat*) about two feet long. It was applied quite often and was not purely a symbol of discipline and authority. 'Spare the rod and spoil the child' was a biblical quotation that was interpreted literally. Cruelty and kindness were the ultimate in penalties and privileges – the one complementing the other. Our betters were capable of cruelty in administering penalties, often with little justification. That was how we felt about it, anyway, at the receiving end. The dignity of both punished and punisher suffered, but ruling by fear was convenient, albeit less effective than ruling by love.

A wire pulley fitted across the kitchen over the fireplace and it was seldom without clothes being dried and aired. In wet weather, it was used for drying clothes, and as there were no wringing or drying machines, other than Aunt Mary, there was a constant and unpleasant drip on such occasions despite the manual effort to prevent it before hanging up the washing. There was less discomfort to sit and suffer in a draught away from the fire than have some heat and 'Chinese punishment' into the bargain.

A twin-wick lamp with a pretty pastel globe and, suspended from the ceiling, a hanging bookcase and two shelves stacked with earthenware, completed the inventory of kitchen stock. Peat and firewood were kept in boxes under the bench, as were the boot last and the repair box for footwear. Additional firewood found its way into a large box on one side of the hearth. It had a cushion and was used as a fireside seat. Cooking pots, pans and griddle found their niche below the trestle for the freshwater cask in the lobby, immediately behind the front door. Here also, beside the trestle, hanging unobtrusively in a corner, was the baking board with its three raised sides (*clàr fuine*). Sometimes when the stock of meal was low, it found its way into the kist together with the brush made of feathers (*badag*) which was applied so deftly by all housewives to remove surplus oatmeal from the bannocks and from the baking board after use.

The kitchen floor was made of cement and was anything but attractive. The odd pothole appeared and I recall an occasion when a mixture of cement and cow's dung was used as a filler. According to an old wives' tale it had curative qualities and reduced the 'whoop' in whooping cough. Well, we caught the dread affliction shortly afterwards and there was plenty of whoop to discredit that yarn. After the whooping had run its course the house was fumigated and the disinfectant no doubt killed off any bugs in the dung! In the sixteenth century launderers were said to have kept collars spotless with the application of a mixture of cow dung and nettles! It was claimed that this unsavoury facepack lifted the dirt from the finely embroidered lawn and cambric collars which were so popular in those days. The smell was overcome by a final application of choice herbs. Strange to relate, in recent times cow dung has been used on a house in Hillingdon to tone down the bright pastel colouring of the walls.

The blend was effective in our kitchen in Torran but the ever cold floor still lacked aesthetic appeal. As we grew older, my sister became increasingly conscious of the bareness of our surroundings, and by enlisting the help of cousin Donald various scatter rugs appeared, and we were all more comfortable in residence!

By the latter half of the thirties the slow upsurge in industry gave some benefits to crofting communities and we in

Torran were not alone in doing something about improving living standards. Waxcloth was in demand, especially as housewives realised that it would cut down on the cleaning of floors. The frequent use of wax polish, as some of the women became more house-proud, resulted in a few slips, but the day of fitted carpets was a long way off. Lamps with wicks gave way to 'Tilley' and 'Aladdin' and Primus stoves were a useful addition to the kitchen stock for the preparation of the morning pot of tea.

The byre, barn and henhouse were all in one building which was sited in close proximity to the dwelling house. This was the case on most crofts. With us, the byre and henhouse were at least the farthest away! These outhouses had been built on the ruins of crofters' houses that had been sacked after the Jacobite Rising of the '45 and in some cases following the sacrilege of the Clearances, when whole families were evicted to the far-flung corners of the 'Empire', having been deprived of their land to make way for sheep. The BBC televised programme in September 1988 – *The Blood is Strong* – gave a vivid picture and account of the stress and hardship experienced by crofters.

A corner of the barn was reserved for an assortment of creels, lobsterpots, spades, Highland hoe (*croman*), hand plough (*cas chrom*), peat iron, pick axe and paraffin. On a ledge above, nestled an assortment of tins – tar, paint including that for marking sheep, grease, cod-liver oil, seal oil and a large tin box containing a hammer, an axe, pincers and a variety of screws and nails. Nothing for which a use might be found was thrown away. Further overhead on beams were bags of wool awaiting dispatch to the Scottish Woolgrowers. Tied to the beams was a long wooden ladder. It was home-made and the steps were cut back into the frame. There was no fear of the rungs giving way but the frame itself must have been weakened even if the generous coats of paint and varnish prevented wood decay.

My oldest brother, Murdo, nicknamed 'Luli' for no known reason, planted flower seeds in great variety along the front of the whole building comprising our home and the mission house. An old and somewhat eccentric woman from Arnish, the adjoining croftship, objected to the defilement of God's house, so when no-one was looking and because I objected to her self-righteousness, I planted a generous quantity of nasturtiums (tom thumbs) which I 'found' in the schoolhouse garden next door, in the area of complaint. As a final protest, I stuck a handful of burrs (*cliadan*) up her petticoat while she was having tea with Aunt Mary. At that stage of my life, knickers were unheard of and all the old women wore petticoats and were bustled up. What younger women wore is not known to me.

My second oldest brother, Torquil, was dumb and mentally retarded. I have often felt that more might have been done for him, but we were not in those days in a caring State. I do not attribute blame to any individual: it was the system that failed to cope with social problems of this nature. We were all kind to Torquil; he did not ask much of the world and he showed in his own little ways an appreciation of the considerations that were shown to him. We helped Aunt Mary as we grew older, to minister to his needs. He has since 'passed over Jordan'. My only sister, Janet, was the youngest of the family and she and I were close, sharing secrets to which 'Luli' was not a party. He took to prayer at an early age and we used to find him on bended knees behind a nearby stack. Later, he was joined by Katie, a young neighbour of his own age and for a season both spent some time behind the haystack.

Aunt Mary's son Donald and Uncle Alasdair Mor (big Sandy) whom we all called 'Trochan', made up the household – eight in all. There were two Alasdairs in my father's family and it was common to have more than one male or female with the same name in many families. This came

11

about because the children had to be called after their grandparents, starting off with the paternal side. Two boys and two girls provided an ideal start but it was the age of large families, thus giving an opportunity to 'lift' the names of deceased near and dear ones. There was no end to the permutation, as names could be, and were, doubled up. When sentimentality decreed that a certain man's name must be used in remembrance, it mattered not if the child was a girl: simply by using the expedient of sticking 'ina' on to the name, Donald became Dolina, George became Georgina, and so on. This arrangement fortunately did not affect a sex change on babies at the receiving end. The conversion plan did not appear to work in reverse, but perhaps more females were born than males. The Island of Lewis took care of the situation by doubling up Christian names, as distinct from a second name. Calum Murdo, Murdo Angus and Calum Norman are favourites and woe betide anyone who will not use these names in their entirety. It is a good job that John Thomas has not caught on in Wales. The descriptions '*mór*' and '*beag*' (big and small) were applied respectively to the older and younger person carrying the same name. To the uninitiated the description was confusing, as in many cases the older son or daughter was smaller than the younger! The arrangement lacked imagination but we lived with it happily enough. Some families made a positive effort to produce enough progeny to allow the names of near relatives to be 'remembered'. They often struck a lucky balance of males and females, most of whom were born in late summer or in the autumn, preferably before the start of the harvest work.

When I was about five years old, there were some hundred people living in North Raasay – from Kyle Rona to Brochel Castle. Our family lived in Torran until I was nearly fourteen years of age, when we moved to Oscaig in 1939. Our cousins, who were much of our own age, lived in a thatched

12

house under the *'Meall'* (sizeable hill), about half a mile away. Uncle Donald, whom I have mentioned already, was a fast talker and a real Casanova in his time by all accounts. He too had been a sailor and knew all about being torpedoed. He was an expert maker of creels, lobster pots, walking sticks and heather rope, enjoyed a joke about himself, and was great fun.

Uncle Donald's wife, Aunt Annie, who possessed no mean cleavage, came from the Applecross area. In our naughtier moments we padded our chests and mimed her accent which differed considerably from our own but was still more pleasing to the ear than the Lewis lilt! She kept the house spotless, drank a glass of cold water each morning when, without fail, she got up around six o'clock, and lived to a good old age. She would never eat oatmeal porridge or marmalade. They played havoc with her innards. I can still see the pure white frills of lace over the recessed beds and the well scrubbed wooden covers she always kept over the pails of well water. She worked hard but her day's work was well organised and she had time for a ceilidh. Not for her the reading of novels – Oxendale's and J. D. William's catalogues of clothes and hardware were much more interesting. When no-one was in for a ceilidh many hours were spent by everyone, young and old, perusing catalogues, and to the list can be added Pryce Jones, Forrest, Lennards, B. G. May and Smarts. The last two offered a wonderful world of toys and fancy goods, such as moving pictures (made of matchboxes) and paper flowers that blossomed out when placed in a glass of water. The catalogues were passed around among young and old, from house to house, with a stern reminder that they must be returned. 'Penny novels' had no place in our homes. We first heard of these from a well-informed preacher who told the congregation that they were the work of Satan – hot from his printing press perhaps! In contrast, the coveting of catalogue goodies and the temptation that might be placed in the way of children was a consequence that was continually overlooked.

Auntie Annie's black-and-white mealie puddings were excellent. Another of her speciality dishes was steamed cod's head (*ceann grop*), stuffed with cod's liver, oatmeal, onions and seasoning. It was equally good to eat when sliced cold and shallow fried. Sheila in Arnish, the mother of 'Calum the Road' – of whom more later – put raisins in her mealie puddings, but we cared as little for these, good cook though she was, as we did for braxy mutton. Braxy meat came from the carcasses of over-fat sheep which at the time of 'natural' death were bled immediately! As time stood still for crofters the assessment of immediate death is anyone's guess. At least it was still warm and the crows had not got at it first.

Townships had their own dietary code. The people in Arnish ate braxy mutton and dried dogfish; the people in Torran did not. Conger eel was another doubtful starter. Tormod Dubh (Black Norman) from Kyle Rona was said to have been bitten in the neck by a semi-conscious conger which he was carrying in a creel. My father would not eat eel and we followed suit. Others were not so inhibited and they literally licked their fingers after a feed of dried salt eel. It was of course difficult to avoid finger licking as it was well known that it was only posh people and Sassenachs who used knives and forks for fish. After all, these implements spoiled the taste of such tender food as fresh fish in particular. There was an apt Gaelic saying which was thrown at us when we grew older and developed such heathen habits as a liking for cutlery when eating kippers – '*B' eòlach do sheanair air sgian agus forc*'. Translated it means: 'Your grandfather was well acquainted with the use of a knife and fork'. It was a sarcasm which to a Gaelic speaker loses its subtlety when translated into English. No-one, but no-one would eat potatoes and salt herring with anything other than their fingers. In this way the taste was preserved, so we were told! A basin of cold water complete with Lifebuoy soap and a rough towel, usually made out of a cereal sack, was always passed round after this indulgence. Finger bowls could only have been for those who lifted a little finger when drinking tea!

It was acceptable to drink tea by pouring it from the cup into the saucer and blowing ripples over it for quick cooling. It was a useful device if you were lagging behind and felt that the head of the household, with an eye to the spring work, was waiting to 'return thanks'. Very good tea at two shillings and sixpence a pound was supplied by Macleod's of Edinburgh. For every order of six pounds' weight, a pound of coffee was included with the compliments of the firm. My father, who had acquired among other notions a taste for coffee during his seagoing days, always made sure that tea was on order. This was done through the tea firm's agent, Ian Breugach (Ian the fibber) from Skye. The true English translation is 'liar' (which Ian was not) but as in so many cases, Gaelic is less offensive, though no less effective, as a language. Anyway, it was easier to say than 'a travelling Ananias'! Ian told a good yarn and was a charmer, a talent which served him in good stead as a traveller or salesman in those depressed years. He stayed overnight in whatever house nightfall overtook him. He had a seemingly never-ending fund of stories and his company was always much sought. The following morning he went on his way having secured another order of Macleod's tea!

Ian had a brother, 'Allie Willie', whose acquaintance I made some two decades later. He owned the general stores in Struan, Skye and by that time edited a local magazine; *The Clarion of Skye*. It was a popular and pioneering tabloid, but with a limited circulation and distinctly limited resources. It did not survive. Various anecdotes and interesting articles appeared; and in the early spring of 1957 an anonymous contributor gave a graphic description of his own impressions of the day in 1910 when sheep shearing –

'fleecing day', as he called it – took place. Skye place names like Balgown, Ullinish, Ebost, Totarder, Talisker Head, The Maidens, The Tables of Leod, Wiay and Tarner Islands rolled off Alick's printing press and fell into place in an article which highlighted the importance of 'fleecing day' in an islander's calendar.

Donald Graham and his family lived in the house over the hill in Torran, halfway to Uncle Donald's. The house had been built under a precipitous rock and had a commanding view of Loch Arnish. It had a corrugated iron roof, coloured red. The walls were lime washed and, with a sizeable porch to the front, the house looked quite distinctive. The kitchen which, like all croft houses in those days, was also the living-room, boasted a 'hanging' chimney. There was always a warm welcome with a good peat fire burning, complete with a large cast-iron kettle on the boil by the hearth. It was some years later that enamel kettles became fashionable, probably owing to the discovery of Primus stoves.

Two of Donald's teenage daughters, Ann and Mary, took turns in shopkeeping. The shop was no more than the built-in wall cupboard by one side of the fireplace in the kitchen. The main items for sale were assorted biscuits, most of which were given away to youngsters such as myself, who after the stores – always referred to as messages – arrived from Portree found the vicinity of Donald Graham's house a pleasant place to play!

Donald Graham had a steady hand and was good with his pocket knife which he used expertly to cut whitlows, an affliction from which Aunt Mary suffered. One slash and there was immense relief until the next time. He was a raconteur in a class of his own. As his stories unfolded at ceilidhs he became more demonstrative and, although a large man, the energy expended must have been consider-able. He told us age-old stories which seemed to improve with the telling and could be oft repeated without any sign of boring the listeners. The supernatural, the Water Horse, people and places in Rona where he had lived for a good part of his life, were favourite subjects. His stories about witches kept us entranced, and at such an impressionable age we accepted these yarns about wayward women who turned into cats and hares to suit the occasion and had the power to capsize boats in storms of their own creation by swirling water in a basin in which they then placed eggshells previously punctured to make sure they sank. A Gaelic chant sealed the fate of the hapless sailors who were quite impotent in the circumstances in which they were placed. Perhaps this was their original offence!

Never leave your eggshells unbroken in the cup,
Think of us poor sailormen and always break them up;
For witches come and steal them and sail away to sea,
And make a lot of misery for mariners like me.

Some of Donald's stories which related people to places were based on fact and held our interest even more. One example was the connection between robbers and a landing place in Rona known to us through family conversation as 'Port nan Robairean' (the Port of the Robbers). These robbers of bygone days were pirates – loners who had defied Highland chiefs and were a law unto themselves. They roved the sea, plundered ships, and took refuge in Rona, Raasay and other Hebridean islands. Donald spiced these stories by delving into the patronymics of some person in the locality and concluding that he or she was truly descended from a Raasay or a Rona robber. He could liven any ceilidh, but above all else, he was a kind man with great personality and a sense of humour. The latter characteristic may not have been appreciated by the two 'South of Watford' hikers whom he met on the moor one day:

'Hey Tonald – tell us the way to Rona.'

Donald, in slow English, retorted with the correct

17

emphasis on his own name: 'And how did you know that my name was Donald?'

'Och,' said the second hiker, 'We just guessed it.'

'Well, well – just guess your way to Rona.'

But his stories were not all light-hearted. Robbers led on to raiders, and we listened enthralled as he told us about the Raasay land raids. He painted a picture of pathos, very different from his other stories, so often spiced with yarns. Young men back from the Great War could see no future in the barren rocks of Rona and some, not so young, who had struggled all their lives, barely making a living from poor land patches, resented the reluctance of the authorities to allocate better agricultural land in the south end of Raasay. The coveted croft land was 'raided' by the men from Rona and the penalty for doing so was imprisonment in Inverness for five or six of them who were 'captured' by the police after a raid of their own! It was a light prison sentence of some six weeks, during which time genuine efforts were made at a high level to resolve the problem and defuse an emotive incident which had repercussions reflected in a national campaign not just confined to Scotland. On their release from prison, where life had not been too uncomfortable for them, a heroes' welcome followed, and they, with others who had escaped the clutches of the law, were 'permitted' to settle into their acquired croft holdings in Eyre and Fearns. Donald Graham, in his own inimitable way, said with a laugh that the 'Shoemaker', whose name cropped up often – as the story unfolded – should also have gone to prison! Still, he acknowledged the efforts of John Macleod, the Shoemaker, who was a parish councillor, in doing so much in the cause of equity and justice. There was some emphasis on the contribution made by islanders, many of whom had joined up voluntarily during the Great War. Everyone who was anybody was on the side of the 'raiders' and by the time we had heard the story, which improved with the telling, it all seemed very close to home – more so when we met for the first time some of the 'raiders', who, we soon learnt, were in some cases near relations! Well, on a lighthearted note, 'we can choose our friends, but not our relations'!

Incidentally, much more than we heard at an evening's ceilidh in Torran, about the Raasay land raids, has since been revealed. The file on the incident was opened to the public in January 1982 and may be seen at the Scottish Records Office in Edinburgh. This information appeared at that time in a short and interesting article by Brian Wilson in the *West Highland Free Press*. It confirmed the local slant on the unhappy episode, even allowing for some embellishment and emotional sentiments.

Like my own father, Donald Graham was a widower, who had been left with a young family on his hands. His oldest daughter, Catriona, was the 'housekeeper' and she produced the tastiest of oatcakes. Her father's personality was mirrored in her character and she was so kind to children. James, the older son, who had the misfortune of accidentally shooting himself in one of his legs while handling a muzzle loader, left home as a young man to become a lighthouse keeper. His job took him to Ailsa Craig, the Orkneys and Rona – the latter place being where he had spent a good part of his youth. I clearly recall seeing him early in the morning, saying goodbye to each one of us. He subsequently married Rita, our beloved schoolteacher on whom I had a boyhood crush!

The only fishing boat from Torran, *Isabella*, was owned by Donald Graham. Uncle Donald was one of his crew. Donald, the father of 'Calum the Road' who receives some mention later, owned a smaller boat named *Flora*. My father and Calum were members of his crew. Loch Arnish, sentinelled by Manish Point and Aird Head, with a panoramic view of Skye for background, was often crowded with fishing boats, many from Staffin and as far away as Kyleakin! The world was a smaller place at that time, and fishing fleets from countries such as Denmark kept to their own fishing grounds. Hospitality was always shown to these 'foreign' fishermen from Skye and elsewhere and the evening ceilidh was much looked forward to by us as youngsters. We could listen and speak when spoken to but we were not permitted to join in a conversation with our elders. Gossip must never be repeated. Our sharp ears often picked up juicy details about someone that we knew and it was indeed a temptation to reveal all in the playground to that 'someone's' children. There were other simple pleasures in our schoolday lives to divert attention and we kept all our secrets for airing in the privacy afforded to us at bedtime.

My father was a member of the local Nursing Committee. This meant a periodic visit to the south end of Raasay, some twelve miles on foot. Hiring one of the two cars on the island was out of the question. His journey became more pleasant year by year as he found it interesting to partake of refreshments in Clachan, with Peggy and her aged father. Clachan became a regular stopping place and intimations of Committee meetings were on the increase. Aunt Mary was convinced that it was a 'put-up job', but she, bless her, did not grudge him his new-found joy. Peggy became my stepmother when I was seventeen. Later on, when home on leave from the merchant navy, and enjoying a glass of beer with my father in Raasay House Hotel, I got round to the subject of these frequent earlier meetings, but he put me neatly in my place by reminding me that he too had been a sailor in his time and that 'water under the bridge' was nearly as good an adage as 'ships that pass in the night'.

Aunt Mary was the custodian of a canteen of good quality cutlery which had belonged to my mother and was ear-marked for my sister's bottom drawer. It only saw the light of day when we had special visitors. The pieces were checked item by item after use, not in case that any may have been lifted as souvenirs, but to ensure that none had disappeared with the washing-up water, which in the absence of a plug-hole was always thrown by the basinful over the dyke, just yards away from the front and only outside door of the house. The soapy water was at that stage lukewarm, full of germs and tea-leaves – all very good for keeping greenfly and other plant pests at bay. Water with carbolic was particularly valued for this purpose and I believe that this old practice still finds favour with modern-day gardeners. Tea-leaves were sometimes retrieved and mixed in with the peaty black soil in the pots of geraniums. The compost so formed produced huge plants which were in flower for most of the year.

Torran, like most of Raasay, is known for its flora and fauna. In my childhood days, student botanists headed by Professor Heslop-Harrison from King's College, Durham, paid an annual visit to Torran. There was no restaurant and this mixed group of about eight landed in our house where my father and Aunt Mary showed them hospitality. The 'room' table with its white and spotless cloth, showing off three long and symmetrical ironing lines, gleaming glass-ware and mother's cutlery, was well and truly laden for the occasion. A large patterned glass sugar bowl, on its own pedestal, epergne of our banqueting table, had pride of place as a table centre. It must have held a pound of sugar. The granules glistened and complemented the rest of the table appointments.

A similar bowl now has pride of place in our own 'glass cabinet'. It was given to us by Mrs Christina Clarke, a Gaelic speaker and a neighbour, as a token of remembrance of her own mother, a native of Achiltibuie who had lived in Second Coast, near Laide, a village in Wester Ross, for most of her life and to whom the sugar bowl had belonged origin-ally. The elderly mother, a fluent Gaelic speaker, always called on us whenever she ventured 'south of Watford'. A chat in Gaelic was a special treat. We too enjoyed these visits which, alas, are now no more.

But we now return to the table in Torran, with its scones, oatcakes, pancakes and some large 'butter' and 'Skye' biscuits from the special tin which was reserved for visitors. Yes – there was indeed a brand of biscuit known as 'Skye'. These and the butter biscuits, or, on occasions, caraway ones, were stocked by grumpy 'Post Office Mary' in Clachan. There was also fresh butter, cream, crowdie and home-made jam. The main course was fresh haddock, straight from the sea, lightly steamed and served with a knob of butter. A sauce would have been an insult. It was followed by *stapag* – a mixture of whipped cream, oatmeal and a little sugar for Sassenachs, if so desired. To us as children it was common fare, but our guests considered it a treat. There was no question of payment. The 'bed and breakfast' brigade had not yet arrived in the Highlands and Islands – they never did arrive in Torran! It was Highland hospitality at its best, but it was not the end of the story, as in our case it was amply repaid at Christmas time when a parcel arrived containing a large fruit cake and some chocolates – undreamed of luxuries! In later life, youngsters, including my own, spurned fruit cake and went for the pancakes and scones. Life's wheel indeed goes full circle.

Ceilidhs were not all gossip. They provided an opportunity for getting on with some work. No woman, young or old, would dream of visiting a neighbour without taking along some knitting. The woman of the house took the opportunity to delegate to her female guests such duties as wool carding and wool twisting while she herself would take a spell at the spinning wheel. The usual garments produced were pure wool stockings for both sexes, socks and long underpants for the menfolk. The latter had cotton lining sewn on to the waist band and delicate areas. This occupation by a gathering of womenfolk was the subject of the odd ribald joke over which we youngsters, who had good ears, pondered. The occasional mishap led to a string of expletives (*tapagan*). Their use was the prerogative of women and the expressions sounded much less offensive in Gaelic than in English. The menfolk, visitors as well as the host, found the ceilidh a suitable occasion on which to repair fishing nets and lobster pot nets. It was not unknown to heat and carve sheep's horns for the crooks of walking sticks.

Preparing pipe tobacco was a work of art. The Black Twist or Bogie Roll was sliced into fine rings with infinite patience and care, and then ground in the palm of one hand, using the clenched fist of the other hand to give a mortar-and-pestle effect. The aroma from the tobacco smoke spiralling its way to the rafters was not unpleasant but I loathed the practice of spitting into the open fireplace, which was part of the pipe-smoking ritual. There was an art in spitting whereby the spit of the perfectionist took off at great speed, whizzing into the embers, from whence would emanate a sizzling sound such as could be heard when roasting live crabs on the hearth. It was not so in every case and the mucus that missed made its mark on the mantelpiece or ended up as scales on the outside of the boiling kettle, earning a rebuke for the husband if he was the culprit. If a visitor was the transgressor, nothing was said – the look was enough – and he was soon altering the angle of his chair. I never could understand why spitting had to accompany pipe-smoking, unless it was because of the lack of teeth!

Even allowing for this dampening effect there was always a good fire burning. Peat and logs of silver birch provided a good combination. Willow, hazel and mountain ash, when overgrown, were also cut for firewood but aspen was left alone. We were not told why – but I learnt in later years of the widely held belief that the cross of Christ's crucifixion had been made from the aspen tree.

Tea and home-made fare were always, well nearly always, provided when someone came for a ceilidh. One housewife in the community was somewhat economical with her hospitality – perhaps with good reason. When a neighbour dropped in, the lady of the house would fill the kettle to its brim and place it on the swee (*slabhraidh*), way up above the peat fire. Having given up any hope of a cup of tea, the neighbour would indicate that it was time to be away as the night was cold, wet or whatever. 'Oh my – won't you wait for a cup of tea? I've got the kettle on', she would say in her own charming way whilst going for the neighbour's coat! There were not many ceilidh visitors in this house! The housewife, who was really a nice soul and not in the best of health, came from another place and never seemed to have been accepted fully in the North Raasay community. Her people were said to have had contact with the 'little folk'. It is at least some comfort to her male descendants and relations that in those days a fairy was a fairy as distinct from the more modern interpretation of the term. Suffice it to say that in our childhood days we were happy to accept fairies into our little world. In our fertile minds there were good and bad fairies, and with the help of my brother Murdo, who was good at telling bedtime stories, we fantasised all the way to the Land of Nod. As we grew older, the fairies gave way to memory lessons for school next day. The world was getting bigger and it seemed a more cruel place, even in Torran. Our little lives seemed less secure.

Despite, or perhaps because of, our religious upbringing, there was a strong belief in the supernatural. How could it be otherwise? Many of our elders believed in ghosts and 'happenings' connected with the spirit world, or with those about to enter it. There were some among us who had 'the gift' and could see into the future. Gifted or not, their ability to foretell events would seem to have been well documented. They were not empowered to have a peep and broadcast happy events like weddings and births, but goodness me, there were plenty of sightings of funerals and near sightings in the form of omens. Hammering was a favourite one and was a sure sign that a coffin lid would shortly be nailed down (screwdrivers came later). After a bereavement, the messengers of doom, in restrained tones, let it be known in graphic detail what they had seen or experienced. They would have mentioned it earlier but it would only have upset the poor family. It is remarkable that their credibility was not questioned. My own father and others who had gained worldly experiences may have had reservations, but as children we concluded that the 'grown-ups' around us believed totally what they had been told.

Premonitions, as distinct from the supernatural, are not being discounted, but seeing lights as omens, though not original, was also popular with 'sightseers'. People going to ceilidhs, even with a full moon, took lanterns, before torches became fashionable. The aurora borealis or northern lights indicated pleasure from above, whereas lightning did not. What about the luminous display which on one dark night I could see, through the slats of the barn door, as I made for the peat stack by the end of our house? The peat stack was doused at speed and I bolted indoors blurting out that I had seen a ghost. If this was second-sight, I did not want any of it. Trochan rose to the occasion, made for the barn and returned with a fillet of dried fish – one of many hanging on a string in the barn. He showed me, in a dark corner of the lobby, after I had changed my wet trousers, the glow of phosphorus from the fish. The fillets were packed in a box next day and it could be said that my ghost was truly laid!

Parents had a great sense of delegation. It was our job as children to make sure there was plenty of peat and sticks available for the hearth fire. Every house had a well within reasonable distance and the older children took it for granted that it was their duty to see that the house barrel was filled daily.

Neighbours simply dropped in for a ceilidh or 'in the passing'. There were no formal invitations other than occasionally for friends and neighbours on a visit from their homes in far away places. Relations of neighbours on a periodic visit regarded it as a duty to call on everyone. The odd person who did not do so was branded as 'distant'. There would be much speculation as to who such an odd person took after and the lineage was well analysed, back to the third and fourth generation.

Levels of pride and status could be found even in poverty. The eccentric woman in Arnish had many children and barely an oat to her husband's name. She had an inordinate amount of brass – the real hard stuff – in the house. Beds had brass knobs, the mantelpiece had brass edging, also a brass rail. Stacks of gleaming brass ornaments were on shelves everywhere. The family was very poor but allowance was made for the cost of Brasso. Her older son, in his teens, was off to Glasgow to earn a living. Her parting words were, according to local gossip, 'Now my son, you dress yourself well and the house can whistle'. Neighbours considered this advice novel and rather remarkable as parents always looked to members of their families to give financial help once they became breadwinners. Crofters were all poor in terms of money but perhaps some were more equal than others. Years later, after she was widowed, this old dear moved house to Inverarish, the posh place on the island. She had coal to burn for the first time in her life and she promptly washed it. What dirty fuel compared to peat and birch logs! During the war when crockery was hardly obtainable, she received a gift of plain and rather heavy teacups. Not caring for such economy measures she smashed them and threw the pieces in the nearby river. There was a use for most things, provided they were pretty, and her neighbours were amazed to see curtains on her hen-house, made from fine patterned material which also was hard to come by at that time. It is not known if her pullets became more productive, but Kate from across the terrace maintained that this luxury living was reflected in fowl snobbery and it was observed that these pullets did not even cackle after laying oblongs.

The girls during most of my childhood wore long hair, long woollen stockings and tall boots of a type that are back in fashion from time to time. My sister started to sport short stockings, a present from a maternal aunt who lived on a farm near Nairn and did not have too much in common with her husband. Janet's knees were exposed and 'Panac' from over the hill got into her stride about the immodesty of the present generation and found various texts in the Bible to support her shallow argument; one always can! She reduced Aunt Mary to tears but did not win, and in next to no time short stockings gave way to socks – very American indeed! It reminds me of the wartime joke about skimpy 'utility' skirts at the time when GIs all but swamped Clydeside. 'One yank and it's off' was a standard laugh-line in the St Georges Road Playhouse; and who could say it better and get away with it, than the well-loved comedian, Lex Maclean?

Long hair invited nits and the visiting school nurse set up searches and had a field day. The remedy was a generous dousing with paraffin followed by a good hair wash using Lifebuoy soap which was always in plentiful supply. There were no modern-day shampoos. Few suffered from dandruff and 'Head and Shoulders' simply meant that you kept these parts of your anatomy straight and looked the world in the eye. The girls certainly had to suffer in order to preserve their long tresses. Was not long hair, so said the Scriptures, 'a woman's glory'! Wild beasts, domesticated beasts and birds, also cod when not in season, all carried ticks and lice. Creepy crawlies were around us. Living conditions, with so much animal life about, encouraged vermin. Fresh air and soft rain acted as antidotes, baths being confined to the extremities. The washing of hands, arms, face and feet bordered on the fetishistic. Burns' 'Address to a Louse' may have made the creature more socially acceptable, but in fairness to island crofters of those days there was a good standard of body cleanliness. There were of course some fleas and flies but standards of cleanliness and hygiene were much higher than in many city areas of Great Britain. It says a great deal for the awareness and care taken both by parents and teachers. Hygiene after all is what Sassenachs put in soup!

Boyhood days in Torran were never dull. Mid-April to the end of September marked the time of year when we were allowed to go barefoot. The saving in boot leather must have been a relief to parents but they gave no indication of their thinking, and permission to go barefoot had to be sought. It was given with some qualifications and reservations but there was a mutual understanding, so to speak. Feet were washed nightly with a generous application of carbolic, Lifebuoy or Sunlight soap, and they were well dried with a hessian 'towel', which probably had been used earlier after a meal of salt herring and potatoes! (Linen flour bags, incidentally, were bleached, perhaps to remove the name of the manufacturer, and then used as pillow covers. They lasted forever.) Limbs suffered the odd cut but toes suffered most, following an argument with embedded stones. Outdoor games such as hide-and-seek also led to mishaps. I fell and broke a front tooth and, being somewhat vain, had it replaced in my early teenage years on my first ever visit to the dentist, Mr Harvey, who had his practice in Portree. On another occasion I slipped in a brook and acquired a big gash on my left leg. The scar is still there and has of late irritated me! I got home and sat by the fireside in some pain, doing my best to hide my injury from Aunt Mary. It was not to be. It would seem that I was regarded as rumbustious and my silence implied that there was something to investigate. A quick look revealed all and to start off with I was given a verbal scolding which drew short of a physical one. The kettle was boiled and when some cotton wool had been retrieved from the tureen on the top shelf in the kitchen, the wound was bathed and given a liberal dose of iodine which on contact had me screaming. Like castor oil for internals, iodine was the first line of defence for injury to externals. Pillow slips which had given long service were not discarded but cut into strips for bandages. A piece of red lint, plain side to the wound, with a good spread of zinc ointment, was put in place and kept there with many twirls of the special bandage. The healing process was remarkably quick, helped by some Germolene from 'Big' Sheila in Arnish. She said, rightly, that the wound should have been stitched. I had visions of the sewing box appearing and all but fainted. Aunt Mary, like most of the older folk, needed glasses for close work and her hand could be steadier – nothing whatever, let me hasten to add, to do with 'the bottle'. Few of her generation had their eyes tested. Spectacles were often shared and because they were in so much demand by more than one member of the family, they sometimes got broken, like teeth and the Ten Commandments.

On another occasion, my sister, then aged five, and I helped ourselves to spoonfuls of home-made jam from the cupboard on the stairhead landing. My sister slipped and rolled all the way down the bare wooden staircase, through the lobby and finished up like a rag doll under the kitchen table. Aunt Mary, who had been spinning, jumped across, knocking over the spinning wheel in her wake, seized Janet and on the spur of the moment spanked her! It was only then that she realised my sister was in a state of shock, after which she could not have been more caring. The quick spanking probably arrested hysterics but my aunt could not be expected to appreciate these finer points of psychology. Janet came to no harm other than a sore tummy due no doubt to a surfeit of jam. I was accused of having pushed her but I threatened to tell father, who was at a wedding with

Luli, that she had spanked my sister without cause. I kept out of line of the birch rod which I could see poised at the end of the mantelpiece and the incident was over. The jam inquiry came later!

It has to be said that Aunt Mary's attitude in circumstances such as I have related was due to a nervous reaction and not from a wish to be cruel. She felt that she was responsible for our welfare, left as we were without our own mother. She was close to us; we were fond of her and she showed us many considerations which became more obvious and appreciated by us as we grew up. It was very much in evidence during the winter of 1936 when my father nearly died as a result of blood poisoning from a fishbone which lodged in a finger. The old doctor from Broadford, Skye, was not a believer in anaesthetics. Auntie Mary was distraught until my father's return home when it was Hall's wine for him with everything!

Oatmeal and flour came in 140-pound bolls. These had to be carried on one's back from the steep shore. They were fastened with a rope round the shoulders and women also did their stint as 'Shanks's pony'. Mary from Arnish, then a mere twenty years of age, was as strong as a horse and could beat the men up the incline. It was not considered the done thing to rest until the main track was reached, but Mary did not stop and for good measure she picked up a few kindlings within reach, on her way home to the meal kist. Cells and chromosomes did not worry Mary; she was quite a girl and all her chromosomes must have been of the XX variety!

As we grew older we did our share of tending the cattle so that the patches of oats and potatoes which dotted the hillsides could be preserved. Animal manure in its rawest form, rotten black seaweed and fresh red seaweed, had to be carried in creels to these land patches as fertilisers. We had to lay them in alternate trenches turned over by the *cas chrom*, a curiously shaped implement, not unlike the sign of the square root. It was worked by foot and arm leverage and was a job for the menfolk, although the women of Fladda gained a reputation of prowess in its use. Crofting was hard work but there was a wonderful community spirit.

The townships of Brochel, South Arnish, North Arnish, Torran and Kyle Rona combined their labour resources, like a 'workers' cooperative', for potato planting, seed sowing and raking, in the spring. It was all very informal and there was a repeat performance in the autumn with potato lifting. A neighbourly helping hand was given with haystacks or cornstacks to an older or less fortunate crofter. One old fellow, although often on his benders, in addition to the pre-scribed twice daily ritual, was something of a lead-swinger and forever in the lurch when it came to land husbandry. Never mind, the young and not so young always baled him out. The hard work did not eclipse a degree of humour, particularly among those who were not the immediate relatives. It was a strongly held belief that relatives should not be criticised by relatives, at least not in public. It was not unusual to be reminded when making some unfavourable comment, however trivial, 'Ach, remember that Seumas is my cousin.' The definition of relations extended to third cousins if it suited the situation. In a small closely knit community everyone other than the school-teacher was related one way or another, so it was convenient to be able to draw fine lines of distinction. The rebuff was met by 'Oh well, Seumas is more related to me than to you.' If this was challenged, the relationship might be asserted to be on the side of the marriage partner and in quick time the small-talk took a turn and reverted to the changing weather and perhaps the immediate need to feed the hens.

Small-talk about family relationships, as like or not, came up again over a *srùbag* (cup of tea) at a ceilidh and the shortcomings of Seumas as a crofter were laid bare in hilar-ious fashion. True incidents and gossip were well embellished

31

but there was no animosity; it was all laughed off. We children listened and were dumbfounded at the duplicity of our elders. One old woman who had taken to the high life and sinned aplenty in her younger days had been ostracised and lived in Glasgow for many years: but old age brought repentance and a longing for the Raasay Sound. On hearing that she was coming to Raasay at the Glasgow Fair, Panac in her own uncompromising way said it all: 'So she is still in the land of the living, with so many better ones gone before her; if Calum my late lamented husband had known she was still alive, he would have gone to her funeral.'

Sheep shearing, sheep tarring and peat cutting were also community events. Sheep shearing and peat cutting claimed the novelty of picnics on the moors with well brewed tea served from an outsize iron kettle. Sheep tarring took place in the barn although in my earlier years the 'kitchen' was cleared of its furniture and used for this purpose! It was a job for a long winter's night and the kitchen was warmer than the barn. Tar and a certain brand of grease were applied to the skin of the sheep in alternate partings of its fleece. This dirty work was done with both men and sheep on trestles, the type sometimes still used for sheep shearing. It preceded the dipping of sheep, now a legal requirement, and the object of the exercise was to curtail maggot. When sheep dipping became law, the regulations were not always understood, or conveniently not complied with, in such places as Arnish. Old Calum the Brae who was the precentor in the church, and was regarded as a good-living man, had sheep. Shortly after dipping became law, his nephew by marriage, being something of a prankster, was forever playing tricks on Calum and his wife Panac. One day in the late afternoon he called at their house dressed as a policeman. He was met at the door by Panac who went into a rare panic and, in reply to the policeman's questions, informed him sharply that the sheep had indeed been dipped within the time prescribed by law. On pressing her that he must see her husband as head of the household, she made quick time up the stairs, leaving her rheumatics behind, disturbed his afternoon slumbers and told him what she had said to the policeman. 'Well, well,' said he piously, 'if a lie had to be told it might as well be a good one.' The sequel to this incident is not on record but by the time Panac reappeared downstairs, the 'policeman' had vanished.

The tarring of sheep was a job for the menfolk. The women got together, a fire was lit in the 'room' and there was a good spread of food, including the much cherished fruit dumpling steamed in its cloth with its soft crust just waiting to be eaten! There was also a dram, all the way from Portree. It was never watered, be it malt or blend, and the women only took a sip. A sip was large or they were good actresses because it 'went to their heads' – and in quick time; then the fun started, much to the amusement of the tarrers. Treacle got confused with tar and dried fruit with sheep droppings – good harmless fun – but I am sure that Ian Handy got his own back in more ways than one. He came from Fladda, had been crippled in the Navy and was forever playing tricks. He was popular with everyone and a great sport. He was married to the missionary's daughter and this, so it was said, had cramped his style somewhat. Anyway, he had known her for some time before that event and he was impulsive. The diversions caused by a dram or two on such occasions as sheep tarring were regarded as innocent ploys, which indeed they were. No one got drunk as spirits were not available on such a generous scale. None of the children, not even the older ones, were given as much as a tasting but we made up for it with plenty of fruit pudding and Cheshire cheese, the latter being an acceptable change from crowdie.

The one and only wedding celebrated in Torran during my younger years was in January 1937. Donald Graham's oldest daughter, Catriona, and Donald Macfarlane Macleod

– the youngest of the 'raiders' and one of those who in consequence had been a guest in one of his Majesty's rest homes – were married in the late afternoon in Brochel Castle; not actually in the Castle which has for many years been non-residential, but in the home of Catriona's cousins. Great was the excitement, among elders as well as youngsters. The wedding feast (*banais*) was held in the bride's home and the pre-wedding activity seemed endless. The groom had called on the bride's father days before the wedding to ask for his daughter's hand in marriage. It was part of a tradition, supposedly to reconcile the two families (*réiteach*), and was the occasion for a social evening. Children were not allowed to be present but we had read about it in our Gaelic school books and were content to await the wedding feast.

By the time the wedding procession reached Torran, on foot all the way from Brochel Castle, it was dusk. Periodic shots, echoing through the rocks, fired by some of the young males in the procession, as was the custom on such occasions, heralded the near arrival of the wedding party. Although past four o'clock, the 'scholars' had instructions from the school-teacher, Alexandrina Macdonald, to stay put and welcome the passing party. This we did with gusto, as only children can do, and the only school flag – the Union Jack – together with the school-teacher's best bedcover and a tablecloth, flew and fluttered beside the stone dyke which bordered the school. As the procession moved on, some of us broke rank and were ahead at our own house to give a further welcome. We made sure of this by the simple expedient of tying securely the big iron gate which crossed the footpath near the church door, thereby causing a little delay, during which time we nipped over smartly by way of a short cut across the burn, to our front door!

The wedding feast was in full swing. Everyone in the place had been invited, including the children, and everyone who could do so, attended. Space created its own problems but who cared! The children were for the third sitting, and what a spread! Aunt Mary, Aunt Annie and Sheila from Arnish were the 'head waitresses', complete with home-made head bands such as some waitresses still wear, and they were in fine form. They had helped with the plucking, drawing and cooking of poultry in good time for the occasion. The bride's father was a dab hand at slaughtering and there was also plenty of cooked mutton, supplemented, with a thought to variety, by Fray Bentos corned beef. It was a cold night and a hot plate of broth was a suitable starter. Accompanying the meat, which was served cold, there were tureens of hot floury potatoes and a vegetable which some of us had not seen or eaten before – tinned peas! Fruit, custard and jellies finished off a wonderful meal. Cheese was on the table but we were either too full or too shy to eat it. We were on this very special occasion allowed a sip of whisky to toast the bride and groom, who sat at the top of the table through all the sittings. If there were any demands by the calls of nature, neither of them showed any physical discomfort! Their presence made us feel wanted and important. Catriona, as always, had a kind word for every-one, and the groom, who also acknowledged and spoke to us, really went up in our estimation when, later on, he sang a song 'An téid thu leam a Rìbhinn Òg?' ('Will you come with me young maiden?'). I was to hear part of this song years later and in different circumstances – and not sung nearly so well!

With the feast over, every nook and cranny filled up with the guests for the ceilidh, although no-one referred to the social evening which immediately followed the wedding feast, as a ceilidh. It was a *banais*, however a wedding break-fast might be defined, and the proceedings were in Gaelic. There was drink in moderation, by way of whisky, but no heathen refreshments such as beer. There was no dancing, probably due as much to the lack of floor space as to the

35

absence of a piper or melodeonist (accordions came later). The emphasis was on singing and there were plenty of songs, light, humorous and with a chorus in which everyone could join: they did so with gusto. Songs with a love theme were in demand and unfurled handkerchiefs, shared by couples, kept time with the roll or beat of the chorus. There was also an occasional 'borderline' song and one – a 'traditional' with swing – was rendered by Domhnull Beag (wee – or little – Donald) to great acclaim, 'Loisg a' chailleach a camus air eibhleag – Chuireadh i feum air ola na ròn'. The song theme was that an old woman had singed her *camus* on a cinder and was in much need of seal oil. The crudity was lost in the lightheartedness of the verses and the sly leer and wink of the singer added to the hilarity. The reader, if not a Gaelic speaker, may at this point, if not good at guessing, refer to Dwelly's or Macalpine's dictionaries. I memorised and repeated, in innocence, the catchy chorus next day and received from Aunt Annie a shocked scowl which soon turned into a grin. Well, I was twelve! From then on it was for the playground audience – out of the teacher's earshot.

Ours had been a memorable evening. Thoughts of my father in Broadford hospital with a poisoned finger were not far away; but they would keep for another day. We lived for the moment, and thanks to the consideration of our teacher – herself an old maid – the morrow was a holiday. Although invited, she did not attend the festivities, as she was a church member – in full communion.

On one occasion cousin John and I misappropriated some whisky which we found buried in the oatmeal chest, which was also the repository for the steam iron and household knives. It was claimed that the oatmeal prevented the blades of the knives, which were not stainless, from getting rusty. We mixed the whisky with chicken feed, having taken the precaution of making up the bottle to the level at which we found it! – and had great fun watching the hens go dizzy. Luli told Aunt Mary who told Auntie Annie, and both of us were 'given the rod' – a bit of foul play.

The crofters in Fladda made their own porter – a kind of stout – which no doubt came in useful for special occasions, but they were not averse to a 'dram'. The young men of Fladda were very good at helping my father on such occasions as sheep tarring. Unfortunately, by the time that I was about five years of age, friction had developed between those living in Arnish and those from Fladda, and further reference is made to this in another chapter. Those who created this friction have long since passed away but they did the community a great disservice and contributed to the depopulation of small croftships. Young people who left did not wish to return and live in crofts surrounded by schism. It convinced me as I grew older that the sin of self-righteousness is indeed a crime.

We often visited Fladda, as there were youngsters with whom we could play. Until I was eight years old there was no school in Fladda, and parents had refused to send their children to Torran school, pleading a right to have their own school in Fladda. Catriona Bheag (little Catriona) who lived with her ageing mother in one of two thatched houses and always gave visitors boiled eggs which were no more than coddled, acted as a voluntary and unpaid teacher until a school was established. She did a marvellous job, and Morag Ferguson from Stockinish, Harris, who was appointed to the teaching post, must have been pleasantly surprised to find that her pupils could already speak, read and write English as well as Gaelic. Catriona was one of the silent minority who contributed so much to the social and cultural structure of a community without thought of personal aggrandisement.

When I was about four years old, Catriona did house-keeping work for the Torran school-teacher, 'Ginger James'.

I soon found my way to the schoolhouse door where I was the recipient of a 'piece' (usually a scone with butter and jam). Aunt Mary wished the practice discouraged and had the bright idea of placing fish heads, for which she knew I did not care, over the gate which I had to open on my way to the schoolhouse. Catriona's heart ruled her head and when no-one was looking, the fish heads landed in the culvert below, to be carried along by the babbling brook to the open sea from whence they came. My piece plan was thus preserved, but only for a season. Corporal punishment was the ultimate deterrent – and it was used!

Fladda is a tidal island and part of our plan, when paying a visit, was to forget conveniently about the tide in the hope that we might stay on Fladda overnight. In this we were thwarted more than once and dispatched quickly by rowing boats across to the Torran side. We enjoyed these visits tremendously. Food had to be eaten as a matter of courtesy in each of the five houses, but our Torran potatoes were far more floury! One woman in Fladda made oatcakes just like biscuits. The other housewives were far too free with the baking soda and the oatcakes looked sickly green in texture and left one with rather a sharp tongue. A favourite dish was caragean made from a delicate seaweed which was dried in the sun. It was served with whipped cream in great quantity. Bellag Handy was forever blethering about this and that, with a religious theme never far away, but she had a good heart and like the rest of the Fladda ladies, was very kind. The only drawback was that they all had balls of camphor everywhere and the smell was quite overpowering. It all came back to me years later at a 'Burns Nicht' concert in the Festival Hall, London, when an elderly lady sported a fur-type coat which reeked of camphor. I said in my own forth-right way, as we moved down the foyer, that I smelt camphor. She, poor soul, close beside me, tightened her coat and moved on quickly with her companion. Camphor suggests moths which no lady would wish to admit as having elbow room in her house. What price the preservation of fur!

Fladda had one fishing boat, appropriately named *Fladda Maid*. My father was a member of the crew at one stage but not when she hit a rock off Manish. Those in Fladda, like their neighbours in the north end of Raasay, bought their 'messages' in Portree. The *Fladda Maid*, contrary to what some said, carried no wet provisions other than paraffin, until she sprung a leak when off course. Fortunately there was no mishap to those on board other than getting wet. The boat was repaired and gave long service afterwards.

The people in Fladda lived rather well, enjoying bacon, sausages and other goodies more frequently than was the case in Torran and Arnish. At school, we played 'shops' during the lunch interval. This world of make-believe had to have customers and my sister, cousin Chrissie and Betsy Cumming did admirably as the Fladda maids. They kept their money – cockle shells actually from Fladda – together with their jewellery, which again consisted of coloured pebbles and little 'pearls' retrieved from the cockle shells, in a tin box. This was supposed to be a chest which, it was said at more than one ceilidh, had been found full of money near the little island of Grianisgear, by someone from Fladda many years ago, and his relations had been living on the proceeds ever since! As children we were quiet listeners who knew a good story, and whilst we repeated nothing, at least within earshot of our elders, it was not unknown for children to have casual exchanges within the confines of the school playground.

Although there was a diminishing number of children as the years went by, we played other games such as our own version of rounders and shinty. The shinty sticks were made of local hazel or willow. The girls joined in the fun so I suppose it all ended up as a composite of shinty and hockey.

The boys always carried a pocket-knife and most were

adept at making whistles from willow. We were shown how to select and cut willows and hazel for creel making. One sharp cut did the trick. There was nothing sinister about carrying a pocket-knife. It was only the sheep, more so the male ones, that had something to fear at fank times. A pocket-knife came in useful for sharpening school pencils and was a prized possession, often given by a kind relation on holiday during the Glasgow Fair. Uncle Finlay, who earned his living with the Clyde Trust, was our benefactor. I possess my father's own pocket-knife to this day. It is perhaps remarkable that articles of such intrinsic value should be retained and not used, because of their sentimental value. Pocket-knives are by no means on their own in this category, nor is the retention of such articles a peculiarity of the islanders of Scotland. Chinaware – teapots in particular – is handed down from mothers to daughters until the line runs out and it is not uncommon to find aunts of old-maid vintage leaving china and pottery to well-beloved nieces. Mementoes of places visited were often collected and ended up in the dresser or china cabinet of the parent's croft house. My own wife was the recipient of Goss china willed to her by a maternal aunt. Crofters' wives in Torran, as elsewhere in the Islands, were delighted to receive teapots, jugs and many other knick-knacks from friends and relatives who descended on them at holiday times.

The Glasgow Fair was one of the highlights of the year. Aunts, uncles and their families, usually large ones, came to Mallaig by rail and by MacBrayne's steamer from there to Portree, calling at Kyle of Lochalsh and Raasay on the way. Those who were going on holiday to the north end of Raasay other than to Brochel, carried on to Portree where kind friends with fishing boats shared a dram or two with the visitors and took charge of a lot of luggage. Those going to Brochel left the steamer at Raasay Pier and then hired the shoemaker's car for the twelve-mile run to their destination.

The 'car road' ended at Brochel and anyone going further north had to travel a few long miles on foot. My aunt and uncle were met in Portree by either the *Isabella* or the *Fladda Maid*.

It was an annual ritual and nothing was permitted, not even the weather, to interfere with the arrangments. My own first visit to Portree, at the age of ten, was on the *Isabella* on such an occasion. Aunt Mary made sure that I was well dressed and I could barely contain my excitement. Portree was such a big place. There was electric light, water came from taps, and the shops were quite something to see, with windows bigger than any I had ever seen before. J. & R. Macleod had a big shop near the pier. The shelves were laden with items such as Creamola, Fowler's treacle (any other brand was considered suitable only for the cattle), tomato ketchup, nugget, dubbin, Reckitt's Blue and Rinso. Brasso and blacklead – items always in demand by crofters – were in another section of the shelving. There was a large coil of black twist on the counter, at, I believe, nine pennies an ounce (twelve pennies made one shilling). Prices were not displayed and 'how much is it?' was common shop talk. The shopping list (line) was attended to quickly and a large cardboard box used for packing the 'messages' was treated to a double overcoat of good quality brown paper and plenty of string – articles which were carefully preserved in Torran for further use when dispatching flesh and fowl for Christmas presents to town relatives. The string, which had been well knotted by the shop assistant, was never cut, and opening the parcel with human aids such as teeth and fingernails could test the patience of Job. We stayed near at hand with teeth watering, knowing that J. & R. always included a 'free' poke of sweets.

My father introduced me to the manageress. Miss Brown. She gave me a large bar of chocolate all for myself, but I kept a piece back for my brothers, sister and Aunt Mary. It was

41

truly a great temptation to eat it all, but nature helped me on the way home as I was very seasick. In Portree, I was treated to lunch by the kindly Davidson family and to afternoon tea in Murray's – or was it Beaton's? – Tearoom. I seem to recall that both were sited alongside the steep brae that wends its way into the village from the pier. The afternoon treat was a reward for my future silence as my father and his fishermen friends spent some time in a local hostelry, down at the pier, whilst I was left to admire Portree Square from which I had strict instructions not to move. True enough, I did not leave Somerled Square, to give it its correct name, but I did move. Mackinnon's Bakery was across the way, so I passed some of the time window shopping. It was here that Skye butter and caraway biscuits were made, large as saucers; alas, my pocket money could not reach to these luxuries and I contented myself awhile, breaking the Tenth Commandment and breathing in the rich smell from the bakehouse.

This fine home bakery, complete with a restaurant, is now on another site in the Square and is owned by the Mackenzies, a charming and well-established Portree family who have contributed so much to a village way of life. Alistair, a first-class baker, virtually ran the business when it was Mackinnon's Bakery. In addition to running the family business, his wife Aline and her son Douglas have in turn conducted the Portree Gaelic Choir. Under their baton, over and over again, the Choir gave award-winning performances at National Mods. The bakery products have earned credits in food guides and continue to be of even higher quality, so say some, than ever before. Anyway, they are very good.

It seemed ages before the *Loch Nevis* arrived at Portree Pier. What a large ship – and so full of people! The transfer of passengers and luggage was completed without incident and the *Isabella* was under way, making for the fishing-boat anchorage in the Kyles of Fladda. From there we would be transported by rowing boat, back round Aird point into Loch Arnish and Torran. Aunt Kirsty from Glasgow trundled an unusually large hamper as part of her luggage on this annual pilgrimage. I took some consolation from seeing that she too was seasick, but there were moments when I conjectured what might be in the hamper for all of us, this time. We considered relations from Glasgow to be well-off compared to ourselves. This was far from being the case, as Glasgow dockland was a most depressed area during the mid-thirties. Many islanders seeking jobs in the big city found their niche in the Glasgow Police, the Clyde Trust or the Corporation Parks. A number from Raasay ended up as church elders. The annual return to Raasay, Fladda and many other parts of the Highlands and Islands of Scotland was but a pleasant release from life in 'No Mean City'. Wives and families stayed on for a further two weeks beyond the two weeks prescribed as the annual holiday for the breadwinners, and returned to Glasgow in time for the reopening of the schools.

Uncle Finlay had a camera, so we had our pictures taken without fail. He spent most of his holiday time rod-fishing from a rock at Losaid, not far from Graham's house. More often than not, he caught ballan wrasse (*muc creige*), a fish with many bones but with sweet and tender flesh. We used to think what a boring life Uncle Finlay must be leading on holiday, but on reflection he must have found his short holiday a great relaxation. Aunt Kirsty brought the ingredients for a dumpling. She made it to perfection, including in the mixture chopped figs. I can even now all but smell its rich aroma and taste its fulsome flavour.

We learnt some bad habits from our Glasgow cousins. They introduced us to smoking tea in the absence of tobacco, which was less easy to acquire. No one smoked cigarettes – a bad English habit not to be indulged in at any cost. Uncle Donald, suspecting that his tobacco pouch had been invaded, promptly made a knife mark on the remaining and somewhat diminished piece of bogie roll. On later inspection, the tobacco, still with an identical nick, appeared to have shrunk even further. These Glasgow lads knew a trick or two and we innocent rustics were suitably impressed! When it came to ingenuity, the local children scored hands down. A tent, in the minds of city youngsters, meant canvas and poles. Tent making in Torran was more original and greater fun. A site was cleared in woodland, allowing the branches of the surrounding trees to be interwoven. The trees became permanent poles and when the weave was completed with 'all hands to the helm', the top and sides were thatched with bracken. We were seldom content with one tent and they became favourite resting places when we tired of playing games.

The simple things of life gave great pleasure, but everything is relative. There was no lemonade or orange juice. We boiled birch leaves, sweetened the brew and drank it without any ill effect. Later on, we saw Sheila in Arnish boiling birch leaves to produce a blue dye for wool! Anyway we did not turn green. This lady, a sister of the Raasay schoolmaster, possessed a wealth of information about cures, many of which were derived from various plants and weeds. We learnt to rub dockweed on nettle stings from which we invariably suffered. She would produce medicines for stomach ailments to suit young and old, beast and bird, and was a great believer in medical ingredients such as treacle and vinegar. Cod liver was melted down and the oil used for the cure of common colds. This versatile product also trickled its way into the hubs of barrow wheels. Wheezy chests were given a good rub of home-produced seal oil and warm olive oil. The latter, which had to be bought, found its way on the tip of a warm teaspoon into sore ears. Thread was tied tightly around warts and, it has to be admitted, they soon went. Ringworm, sometimes passed on by cattle, was dabbed with ink and duly vanished. Chrysanthemum leaves, which were profuse in the shelter of our home, were said to cure headaches, if eaten. We steered clear of this one but it is interesting to find that King's College, London, backed by the Health Ministry, has since conducted research into their curative powers. Cobwebs had their place in the crofters' code of cures and were used to stem bleeding from the many cuts and grazes which were acquired during work and play. In consequence, spiders were a protected breed. (A cousin of my own was affectionately known as 'spider' – I know not why but he never struck me as in need of protection!) Loaf heels were steeped in boiling water and used for poultices. When not available (usually because we had eaten them, dipped in cream and sugar) a poultice was made of soap mixed with sugar. It was effective for boils, which were a common ailment, and was always used to 'ripen' Aunt Mary's whitlows in readiness for Donald Graham's pocket-knife slash!

The older generation were firm believers in the medicinal properties of castor oil, Epsom salts and senna leaves. Children are prone to tummy upsets and we were no exception. A dose of castor oil mixed in warm milk was the answer to our ailments. Faced with this mixture one morning, when about six years old, I bolted from my aunt's grasp and gave my father, in slippered feet, a good run around a mucky byre. The chase led back to the house where I took refuge behind the kitchen door. It was the obvious place to be found, and with a pointing finger from Aunt Mary, which I saw only too plainly through the wide gap between the hinges of the door, I was all too soon over my father's knee, not to be spanked, which might have been preferable, but with his two fingers pressing my mouth wide open, I was forced to drink the vile mixture. The older generation could have taught prison officers a trick or two in the art of force feeding! Trochan, my tetchy uncle, remarked that I would be obliged to do more running later in the day. This was true and even more pronounced as I made for the green lavatory over the hilltop. We quickly learnt not to develop tummy aches simply in order to play truant. The garden Netty was not hygienic and belonged to rural England.

There were no horses in North Raasay. My cousin Donald (Aunt Mary's son, from the other side of the blanket) who lived with us was the local postman. He was light of foot and walked to Brochel Castle three mornings a week to pick up the mail and then back again to deliver it for sorting in the post office at Brae, North Arnish. At New Year there was excess mail and Donald had to make at least two return trips on post days. His cousin, Kenny – known to all of us as 'Kenny the post' – delivered the mail from Clachan Post Office to Brochel Castle, travelling in style by horse and trap. When about seven years old, I was permitted to accompany Donald. What excitement! We came to the deer fence. I had not seen such a high fence before and it was so well made compared with the fences in Torran and Arnish: talk about the Berlin Wall! Little did I appreciate that the fence had been placed there to keep people off 'game ground' rather than to stop game from creating havoc in crofters' 'cabbage patches'. The erection of deer fencing was a costly business for the landlord. The arrangement limited foodstock for the much prized deer but the common crofter must needs be kept at bay. It was a clear, sunny morning and the scenery around me was rather different from Torran. The many cliffs, of varying shapes, were spectacular. I learnt that they were sandstone and that their unique forms resulted from wind and weather over many centuries.

Donald walked very fast and I had to run to keep up with him along the steep tracks. What did it matter? I was about to see a horse and trap! Sure enough, within minutes of our arrival at Brochel, Kenny turned up in splendour, the horse cantering along at quite a pace. I recall that the trap was beautifully polished. The horse, probably a pony, was friendly and I was allowed to feed him – honour indeed. It was a morning with a double bonus, for was not that Brochel Castle, stark, broken but still majestic in the morning sun? I was not allowed to visit the Broch, but that was something for another day, and nothing must hold up the post except the proverbial cup of tea. There was a catalogue of flower seeds with pretty blooms pictured on the cover for Torquil Mackenzie, whose house was one of two down the hill, and a letter, judging from the postmark, from son Kenneth – or was it Allan? – who was busy with the sheep in Perthshire and no doubt sowing wild oats into the bargain. We had tea from Torquil's daughter Sheila and large fluffy pancakes fresh off the girdle. Her mother, Mary-Anne, waddled in with a large pail of warm milk of which I had to have a glass after she had given me a warm welcome. She was kindness personified.

Malcolm Graham, her brother and a widower, by far the tallest man that I had ever seen, lived next door. He had a son, Kenneth, who suffered from a leg infection and was a cripple. He was great company and always seemed cheerful though often in pain. To pass the time he produced an array of hand-carved pipe-holders, picture frames, walking sticks, horn egg cups and horn spoons. He sold his wares for pennies and more often than not gave them away. He has long since said his farewell, but 'age shall not weary him'. There were four daughters in the family. The older two were rather plump and well built but they were so cuddly and all were so kind. Both these families were most homely and my sister and I made periodic visits to Brochel thereafter on the flimsiest of excuses.

The Mackenzies had a highly polished and posh High-land dresser. Gazing down at us from the dresser top was a large stuffed owl which we found fascinating. It was so real. I wonder what has happened to it over these many years!

We visited the Broch, the Castle lochs – rich with trout – and the salmon station by the shore. The hut in which the salmon fishermen lived was a great attraction. It was only in use during 'the salmon season' so we made the most of it. It was nothing like a modern-day chalet but it was so compact and comfortable. Big Angus from Staffin, Skye (Aonghas Mor) was in charge. A fuss was made of us and we were not let away without a large cup of tea, a piece (bread, butter and jam) and biscuits. Some forty-five years later, I made the acquaintance of one of Angus's sons through committee work with the Gaelic Society of London. The world is indeed a small place.

The inland lochs, with a natural beauty of their own, had a fascination for us. It was not sea-water and surely they should be explored, especially as they were not too deep – at least in parts! Hand in hand, my sister and I did just that on a warm and sunny summer's evening. Alas! the loch we chose had a slippery bottom and in no time we found ourselves with wet bottoms – and we were wet right through. We kept our grip for dear life, and on surfacing we were gripped even more strongly by Mary, Malcolm's second youngest daughter, then in her teens, sturdy and as strong as many a man. We were quickly stripped and dried in the Graham household. Considerations of modesty were the least of our problems. We had to walk over three miles back to Torran, and apart from any physical discomfort we dared not turn up wet, other than on such occasions when the heavens opened. We were not well enough versed in nature study to proclaim that it had rained on our way home even if it was dry on arrival and indeed the sun had not clouded over Torran all day – a well known feature of summer weather. I would like to think that we were also as truthful as any occasion demanded.

Visits to Brochel were on the strict understanding that we did not go near the lochs. Disobedience was punishable, and we would be even more uncomfortable with the sting of a birch rod about our bare legs. Mary and her thoughtful sisters knew what would be in store and of course there was a vested interest. After all, had not Mary and her younger sister, Kirsty-Anne, accompanied us to the lochs? It was more expeditious to dry up and shut up! In next to no time we were warm, dry and on our way home with marvellous 'pieces' of jammy pancakes. I can still see a vision of Mrs Mackenzie waving us goodbye from next door and giving her usual jovial smile as we increased our pace up the croft path towards the track which did duty for so many years as a road to Torran. These two closely-knit families took tremendous pride in their gardens, which had thick borders of cultivated flowers and well-kept vegetable plots. Fresh whipped cream was served with puddings and there was the occasional pink fish! Everyone was made truly welcome and the people in Brochel were in a class now all too rare. An added bonus was in summer when Sandy Lee, a young cousin of the Graham family, was on holiday and played the bagpipes. We danced according to how the lively beat of the music affected our twinkling toes and had a lot of fun.

Across the sea from the croft houses we could see high hills and a shimmering sand. It was Wester Ross, with Shieldaig to the north, and there was a good view of Applecross. We pondered over what lay beyond.

Time marched on. Kenny's horse was 'pensioned off' and replaced by a little red van with 'Royal Mail' lettered grandly across it. Kenny, who had been wounded in the Great War, as we then knew it, drove the van for years afterwards. He has passed over, but there are those from Raasay, some living in far away places, who appreciated the 'lift' and could recall his company and considerations when they were footsore and on occasions wet. He lived in an age before the Post

Office provided passenger facilities in far-off places and where the older folk have weathered faces 'and the young fair maidens quiet eyes'.

My sister and I also found our way to Kyle Rona where the track from Torran was far worse than the one to Brochel Castle! On the way, we passed Iomochan with its deserted crofts and houses in ruins. Iomochan, situated on the eastern seaboard of Raasay, had seen other days when the community was a lively one. Landlordism made its contribution to its decay like many another island area. About one 'Highland' mile from our destination we had to pass through a dark ravine – 'The Hollow of Catriona's Well' (Glac Tobar Catriona). The stony track took a steep descent through sheer rock, which cast its shadows, and the spot in legend had a strong link with witches. To be honest, we dreaded the place and hastened on without stopping for a drink at the well, as was customary when travelling some distance on foot. We were likewise always glad when we made the ascent on our way home and put some distance between us and this dark dank ravine.

The Cumming family, to which reference is made elsewhere, lived in Kyle Rona and their croft-house was virtually surrounded by a swamp. It was a horrible hole that had little benefit of sunshine. Four of the girls attended Torran school during my schooldays and they – rather than where they lived – were the attraction. Their father, Norman, was the postman for Rona, where, apart from the lighthouse keepers, a family of two brothers and one sister still lived. Christopher, James and Flora were by all accounts a strange trio and the butt of stories that enlivened many a winter's night ceilidh. Norman Cumming had a boat which, as he could not walk on water, was essential for delivering the Rona mail. When I was older I was allowed to go with him to lift the lobster pots in the Kyles of Rona. Although he was a quiet man he had great personality. He pointed out to me seals and otters, neither of which I had seen before. There was a variety of seabird life and it seemed to me at that young age that I was in a different world from Torran. Other than for a horrible smell of rotten fish which was being used as bait, the trip was an enjoyable one, helped by a calm sea and a few large crabs to take home. I recall that Norman had a fair catch of lobsters which he transferred to a storage creel held on a sea anchor (rope and a large oblong stone). Lobster was not proffered and it was not expected: it was gold to fishermen and crofters.

Norman's wife Sheila, or Julia as her 'Glasgow Fair' friends liked to call her, was as rumbustious as he was quiet. Her table was well-laden and she made excellent potted head. This delicacy is made from the meat which is stripped from the head of a sheep, then cooked, suitably seasoned and pressed. While on the subject, a sheep's head was often singed over the hearth fire with red-hot pokers. As a final touch, the eyes were pierced with a poker, and the juice which exuded was applied to give the blackened flesh a finishing glaze. The head was then split and well cleaned, the brains having been removed and discarded. Brains and sweetbreads were never eaten! After a night in salted water, the two parts of the sheep's head were transferred to the soup pot. The broth was very good and even tastier on the following day. The meat was sliced at an angle over the cheekbones, and with its black edging it looked, to us, rather attractive. It was served cold, together with a sliver of the tongue, and was tasty. Aunt Mary did a first-class job on singeing and preparing sheep's head for the cookpot. She seldom ate it.

Uncle Calum, back from Montana, owned Raasay Farm and a car. During the terminal illness of his sister – my mother – he often conveyed the local nurse from her home in the south end of Raasay, to Brochel Castle. From there, he accompanied her on foot, over hills and heather, to

Torran. As time passed, the miles become shorter for them. Love blossomed, and although the sad cause for the Torran visit came to an end, out of sadness came joy and they were duly wed. This itself was short-lived as Uncle Calum died in his mid-forties from throat cancer. During the last few years of his life he kept offering my father a working partnership in the Island of Rona, but he, proud man, did not accept. My father was not particularly good with sheep, so perhaps this also was an influencing factor.

Disconcerting stories reached our ears in Torran in the early thirties. Uncle Calum and others of less substance, living in Clachan and Inverarish, were the victims of thievery. Hay, corn, wool and other outdoor material disappeared in the night. It would not be Hallowe'en forever nor could it be the return of pirates – the theme of Donald Graham's oft told stories – and few people believed in ghosts; fewer still in 'the little people'. Personal goods and chattels vanished when householders were in church. One old lady in Clachan, who deserved better, was distressed to the point of shock. The affair cast a cloud of suspicion over the whole island. The community, despite innocuous gossip, thrived on trust, and the inevitable rumours pointed a finger of suspicion at this and that person. It was not surprising that, as the post brought news of further thievery from week to week, we youngsters in the north end of Raasay viewed the area south of Glam as a place of pirates. Our school games became a version of modern-day cops and robbers. Our 'robbers' were named openly and without malice, but we took care not to disclose our source of information. 'Out of the mouth of babes'! To the relief of the community the thievery stopped as suddenly as it had started. With the receding depression a trickle of young people were finding jobs outside the island and these two happenings were just not a coincidence; so said some who at least thought they knew more than other mortals. The incident is placed on record simply because it left on my mind its own impression of an undesirable way of life. If this kind of unsocial behaviour could take place in Raasay it is not surprising that economic and cultural depression in our cities can lead to riots and a pronounced increase in crime. Unsocial behaviour cannot be justified, but the elements of cause and effect are parts of the pattern of life.

It was 1937 – Coronation Year. The children of Torran school, by now all seven of them, were to be collected by motor-car at Brochel Castle and taken to join in the fun and celebrations arranged in the park of the Free Church manse, near Inverarish. It was a hot May day and great was the excitement as we awaited the arrival of the shoemaker's and Ewen Macrae's cars. Cars were starting to proliferate in Raasay! My sister Janet and I, cousin Chrissie and Betsy Cumming, were in the shoemaker's car. It was driven by his oldest son, John, who kept us in happy and relaxed mood. We thought that he drove very fast! He teased Betsy unmercifully, and even at that early age I detected a glint in her eye.

The fête was well organised. There were games for the children, lots of food for everyone and a tug-of-war for the 'old folk' which we thought very funny. Everyone was in patriotic mood. After the proverbial prayer to close the proceedings, the children collected a 'Royal' mug and a packet of sweets on their way out of the park. The Torran children more than held their own in sport, and the events were talking points for many days. Naturally, it was an ideal subject for the inevitable school essay. No doubt a retrieval of these individual compositions would convey far more sentiment than can be expressed through these jottings. It is unfortunate that life's incidents, as seen through the minds of children, are usually lost at the end of term.

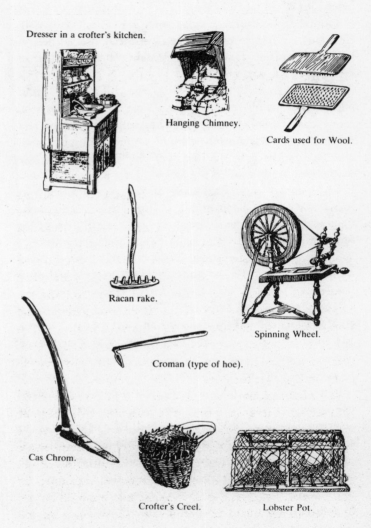

Dresser in a crofter's kitchen.

Hanging Chimney.

Cards used for Wool.

Racan rake.

Spinning Wheel.

Croman (type of hoe).

Cas Chrom.

Crofter's Creel.

Lobster Pot.

CHAPTER 2

IN SHORE AND IN SEASON

> January brings the snow,
> Makes our feet and fingers glow
> *and so on until*
> Chill December brings the sleet,
> Blazing fire and Christmas treat.

Why could the calendar not start with a new season? Spring started in February, which 'brought the rain and thawed the frozen lake again'. We dutifully committed the jingle to memory, like so many other pieces of verse and prose. We were taught in school that February was the first month of spring. Nowadays the month of March seems to have this distinction. It was always so in Torran. The wind and the rain were often with us but the woodland was by then in leaf bud, birds were nesting and the countryside had a lush appeal. The hills, glistening where the sun had broken through a rumpled canopy of cloud, stood over us securely – sentinels of our fortunes.

With the announcement of 'summer time', we were really into spring. There was plenty of bustle by the shore as the rowing boats were given their annual coat of tar below the waterline and inboard. Cracks were filled with home-made putty – a mixture of whiting, white lead and linseed oil. Above the waterline, the wood was scraped, sometimes by using a piece of glass: the curved type so often used by jam and marmalade manufacturers was excellent! After the job was completed there was an application of varnish. The smell of boiling tar pervaded the air and the stickiness of both tar and varnish was very tempting for naughty lads, despite many admonishments should any land on our clothes. Tar had other uses. Sheep were tarred before the advent of Cooper's Dip. It was applied to preserve wood fencing posts and outhouses, presumably being cheaper than paint. Croft-houses were always lime-washed and, in Torran, the mission house and the school house, also lime-washed, looked picturesque, nestling under a background of red rock and woodland and dominated by Loch Arnish casting its many moods and shadows.

We are still on the shore – the phases of the moon were watched and due assessment was made of the ebb and flow of the tide. This was the season for collecting black and red seaweed. The picking of dulse – the mother of seaweed – was a bonus and much enjoyed once its flavour was cultivated. Carageen seaweed was rather special. It was collected, dried with the benefit of wind and sun and used as a main ingredient of a dessert. It was much sought after by the ladies of Fladda. The black seaweed was collected off the foreshore, but boats were used to collect the red seaweed, which involved cutting it with sickles. It struck me as messy and a little dangerous, especially if there was a swell. These fertilisers were carried by creels to the various patches of land scattered all over the crofts – likewise with cow and poultry manure from the heap adjacent to each croft byre and in too close proximity to the croft-houses. Everyone who was able to carry a creel had to help. There was no escape from this chore. Uncle Donald saw to that by making creels to suit all ages and back sizes! It was surprising how quickly one adapted to the farmyard smell. In later years, guano was also used to enrich the soil but some older folk would have nothing to do with it. The dung of the pelican indeed! How could it be in powder form? This was an age before powdered potatoes and soups had been invented. The crystal age may have arrived for the wireless but it had not yet arrived even for table jellies. No, home-made dung, like jam and butter, was best. If providence had meant guano to be used then the beasts of the field would have produced it direct. There was no point in arguing that Torran was not the natural habitat of the pelican.

There were two inlets within the Torran and Arnish fringes of Loch Arnish where the local rowing boats were kept. The shore was very rocky and the boats were pulled above the tide line by the use of wooden rollers made, conveniently, from the surrounding trees. There was quite an art in placing the rollers to avoid damage to the boats, and this art was mastered to a fine point. Rollers were lost from time to time; some local wag suggested that bearded 'Annie Arnish' used them for firewood. Be that as it may, it does seem remarkable that more was not done over the years to provide a better landing place for small boats. Bearing in mind that everything is relative and taken a stage further, it should not have been too difficult to have acquired even a hand-drawn light tractor for pulling the boats, thus saving considerable energy and time on many occasions. It is perhaps too easy to be critical with the benefit of hindsight, a luxury not enjoyed by those who are immediately and actively involved in a way of life. One may conclude that there was a reluc-tance to interfere with nature. It was not laziness. Although folk had time on their side, plenty of unharnessed energy had to be expended on the basic necessities of life.

There were two stone-built 'pens' by the shore, which caught baby fish, mostly lythe and saithe. At ebb tide it was just a matter of scooping up fish by the bucketful. Only those who have tasted fish that has been cooked straight from the sea will know what my palate even now recalls so vividly. Whitebait has never had this effect, however fancy the lemon dressing – and the price. Springtime was still a season for fishing. Herring became more fat and past its best for pickling, but fresh herring, shallow fried in oatmeal, was hard to beat. Very often filleted fresh herring was placed on a hot iron pan, previously dusted with salt, and in quick time it was done to a turn – all in its own oil. Whether this method of cooking was used because fat was scarce, I know not, but it would not be the first discovery arrived at by sheer accident. The catch of herring glistening in the morning sun as the nets were man-hauled on board was a sight to see, and the aroma of freshly fried fish wafting on the morning air is with me still.

Whatever the season, the richness of the seashore was there for the taking. The 'Losaid' at the bottom of Donald Graham's croft was the stance for rock fishing, so much loved by Uncle Finlay at Glasgow Fair time. We were continually warned to keep away from the Losaid. Apart from being a dangerous part of the shore, there was the old cemetery and the cave. The old cemetery had no great pull, as we were worried about ghosts, but to keep away from the cave was asking a great deal of us, as sea-urchins (*crogan feannaig*) were to be found there. Donald Graham had a liking for the contents of sea-urchins. It was supposed to cure bronchitis. We in turn had a liking for the sea-urchin shells. We had such a variety of sea shells that we could have set up our own conchological society, with the details in Gaelic, naturally, and not in Latin! 'Donald Graham gave us the sea-urchin shells,' said we in unison when challenged by Aunt Mary. This, I suppose, was a half truth and we were allowed to keep them. We scraped them, we washed them and we varnished them – an unknown industry in the making! Nowadays, we could make a small fortune. Perhaps there is a lesson here for the new settlers!

We collected mussels and limpets, and after light cooking weren't they good to eat! Aunt Mary pan fried the cooked shellfish in butter. Well seasoned with salt and pepper, the dish was superb and a change from porridge or brose. The limpet (lampet) is an interesting specimen of shellfish.

Whether its sticking qualities are muscular or chemical, I know not, but it gets about! Marking limpet movement was to us an enjoyable pastime. A quick sharp knock removed it from its hold: we spent hours watching heron doing just that using their long beaks to great effect.

Mussels, like other shellfish, were plentiful, particularly in the Kyles of Fladda. Cousin Chrissie had tricked us on an April Fool's day into believing that the load of mussels which she had put, unknown to us, in a freshwater loch on the way to the peats – and which of course she was the first to discover – were freshwater mussels. Proudly, we showed our find to Aunt Mary who gave both us and the mollusc a hard look in disbelief, promptly dumped them on the dung heap and told us in no uncertain terms that we would follow them if we brought any more from the loch. When I became more educated, I got my own back on Cousin Chrissie, and she wasted much time looking for fine gold thread in the mussels' beard, which, I assured her was used in King Henry VIII's 'cloth of gold'!

We were not encouraged to collect whelks for eating. Aunt Kirsty from Glasgow was probably the only person privileged to do so, presumably in acknowledgement of having provided a generously proportioned fruit dumpling at the start of the Glasgow Fair holiday. Whelks were, of course, collected and stored in a large sea bag until there were enough to sell in Portree. After some haggling with the 'middle men' on Portree pier, a price was agreed and the whelks were on their way to Billingsgate. Someone in the family was in for a new pair of boots from Alasdair Clobhdach (Clumsy Alexander). Incidentally, *clobhdach* is not a true Gaelic word, albeit an old one! *Slaodach* or *liobasta* is the Gaelic translation of 'clumsy'. Alasdair kept expensive goods in his shop in Portree but he had good quality footwear and hardware and was prepared to extend credit. The 'Risk' business is by no means new!

On a dull day it was a popular pastime to watch the solan geese (gannets) 'dive bombing' in the loch, quickly resurfacing and carrying in their firm beaks the last vestige of their fish victuals. They never failed to score a hit. We could see heron waiting patiently on a tidal rock below our house. A shot, reverberating in the Cam Mor – the highest rock promontory behind our house – was the signal that 'Calum the Road' had bagged yet another cormorant. He, like the gannets, never missed. Cormorant, or scart as this seabird was known colloquially, was a useful supplement to the cookpot. The bird was skinned and made a tasty dish, provided that the tail-end was cut off before cooking; otherwise the meat tasted fishy. It made excellent broth, which for some reason was invariably thickened with a liaison of flour and water.

Cookery books were not usually to be found in the hanging open-fronted bookcase which was to be seen in all croft-houses, more often than not, stacked with bibles, one or two 'good' books and the inevitable stack of church magazines. Cookery book or not, the woman of the house knew how to neutralise over-strong meat. Rabbit came into this category, and bits of mutton were also added to the stew. Bacon could not of course be spared but ewe flank did very well. Pickled solan goose, known as 'guga' in Lewis, is a delicacy with some Lewis folk, particularly in Ness. By late summer the Ness Navy is established in Suilisgear, which is some forty miles to the north of the Butt of Lewis, and the guga hunters are in business.

According to the *Scots Magazine*, Torquil J. Macleod, a character creation by Colin Campbell, entertainer and farmer, tells us how to serve guga in style.

'Guga à la Back with whelk sauce should be served with running shoes and a 1939 gas mask. [Back is a well-known township in Lewis.] The recipe is said to have been rediscovered on a Macbrayne Ferry to the Uists. Coq au Vin of the Isles. Method – 200 feet of climbing rope, a poaching net, a truss (don't look down!). The guga is salted (and pickled) in a bothan – a resting place for weary travellers run by the Department of Health and Social Security.'

On a historical note the bothan was designed for another kind of pickle. Guga suppers have not yet been introduced to the Inner Cities – a thought for the Highlands and Islands Society of London! Guga has never been in the cookery repertoire of those who live in areas outside Lewis, including the Inner Hebrides, where the expression is used derisively to describe a fat, slothful person, particularly if that person, usually a male, is from Lewis. Women from these parts who marry Lewis men, do so on condition that they will not, ever – whatever else may be expected of them – be obliged to eat guga.

Years ago, long before Penelope the parrot had a part in the BBC radio programme 'Say it in Gaelic', two sailors from Lewis, so the story goes, were at deep sea. One had bought a parrot but shortly afterwards took ill and had to be paid off the ship. He asked his mate to make sure that his mother got the parrot on his return to Lewis. The sick sailor soon got well again and he wrote to his mother to ask about the parrot and hoping she liked it. Mother wrote back, so pleased to hear her son was now well again, *a ghràidh* (my dear) – and yes, she liked the parrot very much – it was lovely with the new potatoes!

Walter Ross, a past conductor of the London Gaelic Choir, told this story, and many others, in his own inimitable way, during pleasant interludes at the Skye National Mod in 1982.

On the subject of food variety, there was the odd deer about. Some of the menfolk were in the habit of staying away overnight and I recall hearing, as a child, about an old man who lived near us and was bedridden, suffering, so it was said, from the effects of a gunshot wound, the result of

61

an accident while deer stalking. We were not to ask questions. After all, food had to be poached in a community which did not have the benefit of ovens!

Who, the reader may well ask, was 'Calum the Road' to whom reference has been made in an earlier chapter? Calum spent his life in Arnish, next to Torran. He lived with his crofter parents until his mid-thirties, when he married the local school-teacher, Lexy, from Dunvegan, and took over another croft in Arnish. His father, Donald, like so many of his generation, had spent some time at sea. He had developed a habit of talking to himself – the result of not wearing a sunhat in the tropics, so said 'Shonny Allan', his neighbour. Donald's wife Sheila was a most capable crofter's partner and with her knowledge of herbs, plants and medicaments, could cure man and beast. Further reference is made to her elsewhere in this book. She looked after the cash and was said to be tight with it. In fairness to her, she knew it was hard-earned and was being careful. According to one of his own brothers – himself a bit of a lad – Donald could on occasion be seen with a wide-eyed grin, brandishing a one pound note and chattering loudly to himself. 'This is one Sheila knows nothing about.' Like the fish, it was presumably the one that got away! A baby girl was born during one of his long sea voyages. In those days sea voyages ran into years rather than months. The little lady had been in the habit of sleeping with her mother. Whenever Donald, attired in long johns, tried to get into the marital bed on his first night home, his daughter kept whispering, 'Here comes that man again, Mammy.' Children have vivid imaginations and they do romance, don't they? Sailors also have been known to pick things up by mistake!

Calum had plenty of experience as a crofter and as a fisherman, having been a crewman on his father's boat, *Flora*, for a number of years, during the time when my own father was one of the team. Calum was also involved with the maintenance of the road, or should I say 'track', between Brochel Castle and Kyle Rona. In the late thirties he took over the part-time job of local postman, which included regular deliveries to Rona, where in due time he became even more involved with lighthouse duties.

As far back as 1925, the year I was born, over ninety adults in the crofting communities of North Raasay petitioned for an improvement to the 'road' between Brochel Castle and Arnish. Some ten years later the track was put into a better state of repair, using local labour, including some unemployed men from the south end of the island. The advent perhaps of 'Youth Opportunities Schemes'! There were no tractors or other mechanical refinements for carrying out the work. It was sheer hard labour with pick-axe, sledge-hammer, shovel, spade and barrow as the tools of the trade. The value of money is relative but the pay was poor and bore no relationship to the work that was done. The track had been widened slightly in parts but it was still not suitable, even as a cart road.

Crofting families dwindled. Calum was active with his pen as well as with his pick-axe. He petitioned and argued over the years for an improved road but was thwarted by officialdom at every turn. By the mid-sixties, 'needs must' if he himself was to survive as a crofter. He set to with a will and a few bowls of brose, and over the years he wore out wheelbarrows, picks, hammers and spades galore. He overcame a little 'local difficulty' which hinged on the ownership of the mineral right in Raasay, gave unstintingly of his time and efforts, and after years of toil ended up with a road, albeit in need of metalling, but with a twelve-foot base, supportive dykes, culverts and sweeping lines that earned praise from more than one surveyor of roads. Calum, by now turned seventy years of age, saw in 1982 the completion of his project. With substantial help from EEC grants, the road between Brochel Castle and Arnish was

given a tarmac surface and suitably restructured where necessary. 'Calum's Road' was also featured in the BBC's televised
programme 'The Blood is Strong', in September 1988.

The deep waters of Tairbort were used by naval craft
during the Second World War for landing services' personnel on training exercises in the rough terrain – complete
with live ammunition. Though little was known of these
activities, any serviceman who took part at that time –
should he now visit the area – would find it hard to believe
that so much could be achieved.

Calum's knowledge of the local habitat was encyclopaedic.
The otter run, the eagle's eyrie and the mineral layers in the
soil around him were but a few of his topics. His other
activities included Gaelic essays about people and places.
These have won acclaim. He was well versed in the English
language and his literary style was unique. During his school
years the school-master was 'Ginger James' who taught his
pupils in Gaelic and had little time for English! Calum
could truly be said to have been self-taught. In the New
Year's Honours List of 1983 he was awarded the British
Empire Medal – an honour well-earned and richly deserved.
Calum died suddenly, aged 76, while working with his
wheelbarrow at his beloved home in Arnish. A cairn above
Brochel Castle commemorates his achievement in the
construction of what has become known as 'Calum's Road':

> No busy steps the grassgrown foot-way tread,
> For all the bloomy flush of life is fled.

We can now return to reminiscences of yesteryear.
Tanning the nets was a seasonal activity. A strong smell, not
unlike creosote, emanated from cauldrons of hot brown
liquid in which the nets were immersed. They were then
hung to dry on cross-bits between poles, their life being thus
preserved for another season. Whilst the men-folk were
engaged in these shore activities, the women-folk were no

less busy. The men-folk did not help them – they were not expected to do so. The sheaves of corn had been threshed by the woman of the house as an ongoing job, before feeding the cattle. It was now time to separate the oats from the chaff, and on a dry day with some wind but not too much, the local women took turns helping each other with this work. Each woman used a big flat sieve (*criathar*). The sieve was as often as not home-made, being no more than a dried sheepskin encased in a circular frame about six inches high and two feet in diameter. It was remarkable how quickly the hens found out what was going on and became over-friendly. I often thought that hens were stupid birds, as I watched them, so it seemed, feeling sorry for themselves, bedraggled and drooping in the rain when they could so easily have taken shelter. Anyway, they were rewarded at this time of year with handfuls of oats and plenty of husk for the picking. The bulk of the oats was in due course bagged, and after school hours we came in useful for carrying the bags to the barn, giving the women-folk time to enjoy their *srùbag* indoors.

Winter was at last giving way to spring. The days were lengthening and the nip in the air was invigorating, having lost the cold sharp bite of the winter months. The glow of moorland fires lit up the evening sky. The flames running with the wind burnt the heather in quick time but did not damage the new growth. Indeed, the warmth generated seems to have helped germination. It can only be concluded that the heat did not penetrate the hill soil to any extent and that the temperature was not sufficiently high to damage the vegetation. Had the flames and the wind been at logger-heads, the outcome might have been different. In the south end of Raasay, gorse, sometimes known as broom or whin, grows in profusion, and after a heath fire it is quickly replaced by new growth, suggesting that the heat acts as a stimulant. As we traversed the moors in the aftermath of heath fires, there was no evidence of bird life having been affected adversely. Truly, the ways of nature are wonderful. Incidentally, the remains of corn stalks were burned back into the soil at springtime. Stubble patches were not set on fire as on farms 'down south', where at such times the environment for suburbanites is anything but comfortable, with noxious smoke and fumes polluting the atmosphere. Once the breeze blows in the direction of houses, housewives are dismayed to find that home fabrics are covered in smuts and ash.

It was now time for the spring cleaning. Here again, the women clubbed together. Mattresses were renewed by the simple expedient of replacing old straw with fresh straw. Few people had flock mattresses. Spring ones had been heard of, but they really were very bad for your back, and man-made material was not natural. Bad backs, of which there were many, were attributed sometimes to the poor make of creel (other than Uncle Donald's) but were not infrequently traced to weaknesses in the line of heredity! A big peat fire was lit near a stream on a sunny morning, to provide hot water – but not too hot – for the annual ritual of washing blankets. They were pure wool and great care was taken with the washing. The blankets were trodden with bare feet in wooden tubs converted from barrels. They were then rinsed dry by twisting over a stick, somewhat thicker than a broomstick and held in position by the woman with the stongest wrist. Other heavy fabrics were sometimes kept in the brook overnight or even longer, with a heavy stone on top of them, to loosen the dirt. The least sign of a downpour was the signal for the woman of the house to make straight for the brook and retrieve the washing; even big stones could become dislodged. Full use was made of the 'beetle' in the washing operation. It was hard work and none too kind to the clothes, but it was seen as an immediate remedy and indeed was most effective. An island way of life was not without its superstition, but that which related to the use of the 'beetle' was lost in history.

Although Rinso had come on the market and was in demand as a detergent, it was viewed with some suspicion whereas hard soap such as 'Sunlight' was versatile and in common use. It was kind to clothes and hands, it lathered well in the local soft water and the formula must have included the right amount of soda. It was applied to stubborn stains, which after a rub on the washboard disappeared like magic. The soap itself did not disappear so quickly – it seemed to last forever. A national newspaper quoted some time ago the story of a woman who was still using hard soap bought by the hundredweight at three pennies (old money) for each one pound bar, by her farmer father, from the West Country. He had viewed with scepticism Neville Chamberlain's declaration of 'peace in our time' in 1938, foresaw shortages and stocked up with soap. It is not known if he confined his long-term purchases to soap, but it is evident that in sorting priorities he believed that cleanliness was a prime virtue; he gave short shrift to cash flow and tying up of capital in stock holdings and he also was a believer in long term investment. The daughter, from her smallholding in Cheshire, not too far from Port Sunlight, was quoted as saying that the soap was 'as good as ever'.

House papering was yet another job. There was no point in wasting patterned paper behind the big Highland dresser. The paper edging had to be cut in those days and playing with the newly acquired streamers kept us out of mischief. Most housewives went in for big floral patterns, but matching the design gave way to the avoidance of waste. The lobby or 'the hall' in modern sedate circles, received different treatment. Heavy varnished paper, usually with squares of blue and white pattern, adorned this area where, behind the front door, could be found buckets of fresh well water, resting on a trestle.

By early April we were barefoot. Somehow the weather seemed, on reflection, to have been warmer in those bygone days. The woodland was polka-dotted with the yellow colour of the primrose, shortly to be complemented by the blue of the Scottish bluebell. Sorrel and shamrock added to the verdure. Buds were bursting all around us and the birds were in trill. It could truly be said that

> Morning has broken like the first morning,
> Blackbird has spoken like the first bird.

Lambs were skipping and calves cavorting all around the place. As a young lad, I had to help Aunt Mary one spring morning with a young cow in a hurry, whilst my father and brother were out fishing in the loch. It was her first offspring. The head and the legs of the calf appeared first, to my surprise, as I did not know what to expect or indeed, do. In minutes, with a heave and a human pull in unison, the new-born beast had made its début and was quickly standing up after a few licks from its mother. Mother care was short-lived and the new arrival was directed to its own stall, previously prepared with a good layer of clean hay for bedding. The experience of calf delivery put me off milk for days and I could never afterwards eat the cheese, regarded with great relish as a delicacy, made from the first milk after calving. We certainly saw nature in the raw.

The birds and the bees were active all around us. Procreation was not dirty. It was all part of our education through observation and the natural process of growing up. We lived in an age and an environment when parents told us nothing about such matters. Had they done so, their embarrassment would probably have been greater than ours! We watched the birds build their nests so diligently in the trees all over Torran. We knew the number of eggs in each nest and felt well rewarded and satisfied when they hatched. It was an unwritten code that the nests were not to be violated. The exception was the nests of seagulls. Their eggs were a delicacy and much sought after. Our parents did not discourage us other than to issue a warning to watch the rocks. In later life, as a seafarer, I was educated to regard seagulls as friends; they were after all – so I was told – reincarnated sailors! I did not feel over friendly towards one seagull in particular which swiped my hotcake, complete with warm syrup, from my dinner plate on a bollard, during my momentary absence to pick up a fork in the galley of a tanker steaming up the Irish sea. Perhaps this feathered sailor still enjoyed the sweet things in life!

We learnt all about the cuckoo by way of school lessons and welcomed her calls in May, but I do not know of any youngster in Torran who actually identified a cuckoo's egg. The cuckoo was an elusive bird and neither then nor since have I seen one. I had a mind's picture of a rather big bird, due perhaps to her powerful call, but my assessment was found wanting. Despite her piracy, I have always had an affection for 'this messenger of spring'! The verses starting 'Hail beauteous stranger of the grove' ('O fàilte ort fhèin a chuthag ghorm') were memorised in English and in Gaelic. In either language there is pathos and a beauty of expression. The song itself, 'Do'n Chuthaig' ('To the Cuckoo') has been immortalised and sung on many a platform in halls and at other ceilidh gatherings. It is one of a collection in *Ceòl nam Beann* (Music of the Bens) – a booklet containing sixty of the best songs in Gaelic. The words and music are in many instances copyright.

We were less kindly to the frogs, and catching tadpoles in swamps and streams was a favourite pastime. Still, the frog population was adequate and the slug population was minimal. We scooped up the frog spawn and 'sold' it as 'sago' in our shops of make-believe. Sago was not our favourite pudding! By the end of April the potatoes had been planted and the oats raked into the soil. Murdo, my brother, as he grew older, developed a keen interest, shared by my father, in growing vegetables. He cultivated a productive patch over the hillock by the church and again displeased the *cailleach* (old woman) from Arnish – of brass knobs fame – who regarded his achievements in horticulture as near sacrilege. It escaped her that 'you are nearer God's heart in a garden than anywhere else on earth'. We were well provided with winter kale, cabbage, swedes, carrots, leeks and beetroot, the last being rather a novel acquisition. Aunt Mary enjoyed cooked beetroot with a little sugar just as she did with her first serving of lettuce and tomatoes! She had a go at using the coloured water acquired after cooking some beetroot, for dyeing wool. It was not a successful venture so she stuck with lichen. It is interesting to reflect again on the eating habits of islanders in general. Few crofters used vegetables other than for vegetable broth, which, with a base of barley, was a meal in itself. Potatoes and salt herring was a staple diet. Not many people were overweight despite the number of scones that were consumed. There was clearly a vitamin and calorie balance, achieved by accident rather than by design. Everyone absorbed too much salt. Ailments such as appendicitis were rare, even although some doctors are of the opinion that the larger quantities of sugar and roughage still consumed by Northerners as compared to the South Country, are related to the high incidence of appendicitis north of Hadrian's Wall.

Potatoes were boiled in their jackets, so there was some retention of vitamin C. Milk, eggs and butter were in good supply and there was ample roughage provided by porridge, brose and oatcakes. Porridge was a thick goo and it was the custom to dip it by the spoonful in a bowl of milk provided for each person for that purpose. Further back in history, there was a basin of milk placed in the centre of the table for common use. This was long before the 'Health and Safety at Work Act'. I was reminded of this historical note years later on seeing Indian ships' crews sharing a thallie for their curry and rice meal! I disliked porridge intensely, and in desperation I rolled the three-legged porridge pot down the slope in front of our own house. Aunt Mary searched high and low and came across a hen's nest in among the nettles. 'Luli', my brother, gave me away and Aunt Mary was very cross, although the discovery of so many eggs mollified her somewhat and her standard ideas of justice were tempered with mercy. The porridge pot, complete with spurtle, produced many more platefuls of 'Harry Lauder's wedding cake'! My father also had no great love of porridge. He pretended to be cross over the incident, but he told me much later that he had hoped my little rebellion would see a variation of the fare for breakfast. It did, for a short season; there was brose for some days and I liked this concoction of oatmeal and salt, barely cooked with boiling water, even less. For some time after my unsuccessful dispatch of the porridge pot there was pronounced activity in the henhouse each evening. The hens were 'tried'. It was quite remarkable how women engaged in this activity could tell the number of eggs for collection the following day. If they failed to wash their hands afterwards, it seemed to do us no harm!

We regarded the hens as scavengers – which indeed they were. They wandered all over the place and had a whale of a time in the dung-heap below the byre. We ate their eggs without qualms and as they were shell-contained we probably did not relate too closely to the hens. Cooked fowl was not over-much to our liking, not because it had the goodness boiled out of it, but because we related it directly to the eating habits of our hens. 'Chicken' soup, on the other hand, was acceptable, as we could see before us an appetising plateful of steaming, savoury broth, generously stocked with rice, chopped onions and root vegetables – truly a case of mind over matter!

Hens are indeed 'birds of sympathy' that cannot even

71

look forward to Christmas. The battery age has stifled their style even further, but – dare I say it? – their food intake, however sterile, is at least hopefully hygienically controlled.

By the end of April the oats had been sown and the potatoes planted. Although raking was a collective operation, sowing the seed was a one-man job. It was scattered by hand, in some cases more evenly than in others, and the person doing this tedious work had to keep moving backwards in the process! Potato planting was a chore and we all had to help. The work demanded that we followed the 'hand plough' (crooked foot – *cas chrom*) used for turning the soil, and placed the potatoes about nine inches apart, in holes which we made with a wooden dibbler (*pleadhag*). In Torran we called it *'plutag'*, which strictly speaking is the Gaelic name for a rowlock or oarpin. But ignorance is bliss and we carried on planting potatoes!

It was May and the days were still lengthening. One of our chores was to feed the hens, after school was over. We had a walk of two miles each way as the poultry had been dispatched to a fenced-in area, over the hills and well clear of tilled ground. It was near 'Fàire an dà Mhuir' (Sighting of two Seas). At that point you could see the sea on both the west and east sides of Raasay. One of our thrills was to gaze, near mesmerised, at the warships which anchored annually outside Portree Bay. The year 1934 was rather special. The Duke and Duchess of York visited Portree to open the Elgin Hostel for boys attending Portree School. We had a school holiday and visited the 'Sighting of two Seas' twice on that day. We could not see what went on beyond the hills of Skye, but we used our imagination and not only was there warship movement but did we not see seaplanes! In 1979 when my wife and I had the privilege of being presented to Her Majesty, the Queen Mother, I reminded her of that visit to Skye. She certainly remembered it and we ended up chatting about all things Highland with emphasis on language and music.

The object of having an annual fowl eviction was to protect cultivated ground. Fencing sparse and scattered parcels of arable land would have been very costly and difficult to maintain. Our elders believed in making full use of their children's energy, and just because we were passing by the peatstacks anyway, we had to pick up creels of peat on our way back home. The eggs were packed in freshly picked moss and placed in the small pails used for carrying poultry food. Fresh moss was also soft, clean and comfortable for body use. Hercules the bear should have included it in the once famous television advertisement. This was the time of year when the tinkers paid one of their visits. They knew that the cattle were in milk and they were partial to butter and crowdie as well as anything else that might come their way.

The tinkers, usually mixed families from such residential areas as Cnoc a' Chrò (the Hill of the Sheepfold), near Skeabost Bridge in Skye, came in fair number, led by Seònaid shalach (dirty Janet). They were not particularly welcome but were never kept at the door or allowed to go away without the proverbial *srùbag* and something to eat. Indeed, they invariably took something with them after much pleading, by way of oatcakes, scones and fish. We children liked these visits and the ensuing begging and bartering which was part of the occasion. The male tinkers were tinsmiths and they produced good quality and well finished pails and jugs. The womenfolk did most of the haggling, all good natured, and a bargain was usually struck. The tinkers were well behaved, and spoke with a lilt that was hard to follow – not like Lewis Gaelic really, despite what some unkind folk have said!

The tinkers who called at Torran and the other croftships were dressed to suit the weather. Contrary to popular belief, and despite the unfortunate label which stuck to old Janet, tinkers were and are relatively clean and healthy. They have

73

their own code of hygiene and as part of the larger gypsy clan some of their practices could leave non-gypsies (*giorgios*) with a thought or two. Dogs and cats, considered as very unclean, are not encouraged in their immediate homes and they hesitate to stroke these animals. They distinguish with some care between utensils such as basins that in many homes are used for functions other than washing the dishes. Aunt Mary knew their ways and obliged by giving them oatmeal and flour rather than baked bannocks. They seemed not to trust food handled by anyone not of their own kind. Others gave them bannocks and they were accepted, but goodness knows what they did with them; I suppose it depended on whether or not they were hungry at that time!

Life must have been rough and tough for them in all seasons, yet they were happy. At least that was the impression they created with the outside world. When the weather was damp, dark and dreary they asked for a night's shelter and usually ended up in a barn. In our home in Torran, I recall them sharing the family hearth, joining us in family worship and spending the night on the kitchen floor. We were none the worse for showing that consideration. Some years later one of the lady tinkers met my Aunt Mary aboard the *Loch Nevis* at Kyle of Lochalsh, greeted her as warmly as she would a long-lost sister and reminded Aunt Mary that my father had made a fine job of repairing her shoes. I knew that my father had not thrown all his sailor's habits overboard but it was just as well that the shoemaker in Clachan did not know of such piracy, even if done as a labour of love. This particular group of tinkers lived in their canvas camp by courtesy of Macleod of Skeabost. They were not educated in the three R's but they were well informed. One old dear, on appreciating that my brother Torquil could not speak, looked into his mouth and proclaimed that his tongue was tied. Torquil in his younger years could emit sound and often repeated 'Ma' many times over, accompanying the performance by smiting his left shoulder with the open palm of his right hand. I have often pondered on this old woman's pronouncement. She could well have been correct in her diagnosis. In later years when traversing the oceans of the world, it occurred to me when docked in the ports of countries now referred to as 'the third world', that we enjoyed a good life in the Inner Hebrides compared with, for example, the natives of Ango Ango and the Cape Verde Isles. Nuns begging for flour, fruit and other foodstuffs on board ship in Tenerife, brought back memories of the tinkers in Torran. The wealth of the religious order to which these nuns belonged was evident in the splendour of the buildings in which they worshipped. Nonetheless, they were concerned with looking after orphans and they did not leave any ship in which I served empty handed. I have seen the natives dive for crusts of bread thrown overboard in Matadi and I was shocked to observe a crowd of coloured workers being treated worse than we would treat beasts in Torran, under the lash of their master in Lobito. The year was 1952. Everything is relative but there are human values to consider as we pass this way but once. 'For a' that and a' that – let's brothers be for a' that.'

May saw the cutting, drying and stacking of peat. It was a tedious and back-straining job in which, one way or another, everyone participated. A special implement known as *cabar làir* (flaughter spade) was used for peeling off the turf. It had a curved shaft and a cross-piece. Like the peat iron which had a long flanged blade, these forged tools required a special knack in their operation – also some strength. The men of Torran seemed to cope! It was common practice, after securing the traditional stack by the end of the croft-house or nearby barn, to leave big stacks on the moorland and collect them by the creel-load as the mood or the opportunity allowed. It was really by way of a hobby later on in the year! But it was an unwritten code that anyone going to Kyle Rona or Fladda left a creel by the peat stacks on the moor, for loading on the return journey.

There were two varieties of peat in Torran, brown and black. The latter was heavy and made excellent fuel. It was nearly as good as coal and the smoke had a much more pleasing smell. It was, however, well over the hills on high ground; but the air was bracing and there was the bonus of a good view. Our eyes were trained at an early age to land and sea movements and little escaped us.

We often met Ceit Bheag (little Kate) wending her way back to Kyle Rona where she lived with her brother, Tormod Dubh (black Norman). She was a friendly old woman, with sharp features, and witty. We tended to think of her as a witch, but, to avoid hot bottoms, we sensibly kept such sentiments to ourselves. She used to sit and rest by a dyke on moorland overlooking Uncle Donald's house, and, having gained an audience, went into fearful detail about future wars and bombs. Had she lived in this day and age she would have been an ideal candidate for Greenham Common and must have qualified as a forerunner for CND.

There was a war going on in Spain at the time, about 1934, and Mussolini was coming into the news. It was all doom and despair with Kate, and we were sometimes glad when Aunt Annie, whose eyes never missed anything, blew a whistle. We knew what that meant. Kate, more than satisfied with her dissertation, found relief behind the dyke where Aunt Annie's eyes could not penetrate and set off at a brisk pace home. Her brother, Tormod Dubh, would then be at the receiving end of her sharp tongue for such misdemeanours as not keeping the cows out of the cornfield or not washing his ears. He was not particularly friendly towards water and gained some notoriety because of his infrequent ablutions.

Later in the year peat-carrying was more fun, as we were able to enjoy a feast of blaeberries which were there for the

76

picking all over the moor. There were also excursions in search of white heather. It was not plentiful but we seldom failed to find some. There was one hollow in particular, past the moorland henhouse and near the path leading to Fladda, which, once found, provided us with a generous patch. A box of white heather was sent for some years to Professor Harrison and his team of King's College, Durham, in appreciation of the Christmas goodies. Reference has already been made to this, but perhaps it bears repeating. Aunt Mary's looks suggested that our motives might be a form of insurance for things yet to come. They were! The parcel was duly posted and the good Professor arrived next year with his party. So did the chocolates and cake at Christmas!

Sheep tending was a regular part of a crofter's toils, in and out of season. The lambing season was a sign that we were into spring, and seeing the lambs 'skipping by their fleecy dams' was a joy to behold. During the summer months I had to 'volunteer' for fank duties at such times as shearing and dipping. I did not care for the method of producing wethers: after an incision with a pocket-knife, the operator gave a quick suck by mouth, thereby removing the poor beast's credentials of masculinity. The method used for the identity of sheep ownership was equally gory. The ears were nicked – again by the use of a pocket-knife – often in more than one place, and sizeable chunks of ear were removed. Like dogs that suffer cosmetic mutilation by having their tails chopped off, sheep undergo mutilation for materialistic reasons. If, like the sheep in Raasay, they are unfortunate enough to have horns, they are also branded with a red hot iron with the initials of their owner. Once shorn of their wool, one or sometimes two daubs of special paint or ruddle, usually blue or red, are applied to selected parts of their bodies – again for identification. The owners of sheep leave little to chance!

The job I liked even less was being involved when sheep fell prey to maggots. The wound, often gaping and covered in live maggots methodically eating their way inwards, was scraped clean. The maggots were literally dug out of the poor beast's raw flesh and tar was then applied to the wound. Although many sheep perished before 'medication' it was remarkable how many lived after treatment, until 'cookpot' day when they suffered the ultimate indignity of having their throats slit and their heads cut off. Either way the sheep was a loser. Sheep drenching did not take place in my young days, and I do believe that many a sheep's liver which made a tasty dinner was infested with fluke!

In the early months of the summer we were kept well occupied cleaning the potato patches. Much of this tedious work was done by hand on bended knees and it was far easier to do, even if more mucky, after a fall of rain. My brother thinned the root vegetables in the garden beside the church, which had become his patch, and I was not trusted to help him. Sheep gathering and shearing took its own course. The women in Fladda could shear as well as any man. There was a youngster in Fladda, nicknamed 'Lovat' in later life, who could identify each sheep by looking at its face, as if it was a human being. I ended up in life identifying the various joints for the cookpot. I had no wish to be a shepherd, and anyway, times were hard and we could not all afford wellies! In fairness I was not pressed to take to the hill. This may have been in the best interests of the sheep!

July was a time for us to enjoy school holidays. There was the influx of relations during the Glasgow Fair. Wild roses were in bloom and it was green verdure everywhere. Other than 'watching' the cows morning and evening and feeding the hens away on the moorland, it was a lazy month. True, our elders were forever on the hill, doing their best to keep the scourge of maggot in check. The sheep had by now been sheared and it was a time for partaking of 'the bread of idleness'.

Hay-making was upon us. There seemed to be no end to the work that hay-making generated. The men used scythes – so did the women in Fladda. Elsewhere, other women used sickles. We children were forever rolling the cut grass back and fore into the sun and the wind. Saturday was particularly hard going as all the hay had to be placed in mounds so that, like the washing, it did not dry on the Sabbath!

Mid-August hailed the reopening of school. It was the start of a new term and it meant class advancement and the issue, in consequence, of new school books – happy days! There was no let-up with the harvest work and, despite devoting time to school homework, we did our fair share of carrying sheaves of corn and hay to the croft barn. When we protested on one occasion after a rather trying day in school at the hands of our teacher, the unbalanced Miss Alex-andrina Macdonald, Uncle Sandy (Trochan) who was not at the best of times known for being over-active and appreci-ated that less work by us meant more work for him, remarked pointedly that we could carry corn and do some homework simultaneously. 'No we can't' – 'Yes you can, by memorising while you work.' There was no answer to that. We continued carrying the corn. What he had said, albeit with an ulterior motive, was quite true. Body and mind had to act conjointly on many occasions when we faced the hard world later on. In fairness to him, he was very bright in his younger days and had taught for a season in a 'side' school in Kyle Rona. Richard Sharpe refers to this in *Raasay: a study in Island History*, but the date quoted may be open to question. I myself would agree that pounding the ship's deck for relaxation acted as the adrenalin for many memory exer-cises. No doubt many others have had similar experiences, although walking may not have been the only catalyst.

The days were still long even although the evening shadows fell earlier across the loch. The midges had arrived and 'watching' the cattle became an unpleasant chore. There was no escaping attention from the midges, with no immunity even on a boat on Loch Arnish. The cows did not fare much better but at least they had a tail for a swat! Torran was vulnerable because of all its trees and its sheltered position. The cows by this time were at the height of milk production. Torran was rich in natural cattle food, so there was plenty of cream for butter and *stapag*, the latter a mixture of whipped cream and oatmeal. Excess milk was left to sour and thicken as a natural process. It was then brought slowly to the boil for the production of crowdie. One woman in Arnish took the process a stage further and made a hard cheese. It lacked the taste and bite that we associate with good cheese and in my time it found little favour. There is no doubt that better quality cheese could have been produced and it is rather surprising that so little local cheese is produced in the Hebrides. Indeed, cheese production of low calorie content that might compare with a well-known Dutch brand should have been possible. Another idea for the 'white settlers' – a new 'Lymeswold' – or for weight watchers, perhaps a local hard cheese with even fewer calories per ounce (or gramme if you must) than the low calorie Cheddar and Cheshire varieties that are now marketed. True, there is plenty of crowdie (cottage type cheese) but it is not produced on a commercial scale. Milk produce was not wasted: sour milk, butter-milk and whey all found their way into griddle scones, which, without exception, were of excellent quality. No-one in North Raasay made oven scones in those days simply because there were no ovens. The schoolhouse, that is, the part of the school building in which the teacher lived, did have an oven but the kitchen chimney was forever malfunctioning so the big black range was seldom used, and never if the wind was from the south-west. The wind on most days was from the south-west! Butter was made by hand, using a plunger, in a long wooden churn, which together stood some four feet high. Everyone who was about took turns with the butter-making and a bowl of *stapag* was the reward. Some even added sugar to it! We had heard of the prankster in Clachan, Raasay, who had put sugar among the cream when his mother was not looking. As a result, there was plenty of cream for *stapag*, but no butter. We can only guess what he got before or after the bowl of *stapag* when cause and effect were discovered.

Later on, a churn with revolving paddles was introduced and it was easier to handle. The leading lights with such innovations were Mrs Norman Cumming, Kyle Rona, Mrs Donald Macleod, Arnish, and Mrs Sandy Gillies, Fladda. No-one in everyday talk referred to Mrs 'whoever'. Mrs Gillies, Fladda, was known as Bantrach Handy (the widow of Sandy) and so on. There is no letter 'y' in Gaelic and no word starts with the letter 'h', so we must put up with the use of phonetics!

The cows in North Raasay answered each to her own name. We had two cows, Nancy and Rita. I asked my father in my tender years, why they were named after ladies. 'Well,' said he, 'when I was with Burns Laird Shipping on the Clyde to Belfast run, I got to know two young Irish ladies by these names so I called the cattle after them.' Happy memories perhaps for father, but hardly a compliment to the ladies.

There were plenty of snakes in Torran and Arnish but they must have been grass snakes and no-one was bitten in my time anyway. However, we were warned to give them a wide berth. When cattle-watching or seeing to the feeding of the hens over the moorland, we were barefoot and watched our step. It was not unusual to find a snake in a warm mossy corner near water, and on such occasions the swish of a rod, which we always carried, made short work of the reptile. Cats also attacked the snakes but I do not recall any of the dogs doing so.

There were occasions when the expected quota of milk was not forthcoming from the cattle. It was a phenomenon that could not be explained. Did the snakes take the milk from the cows? Piracy of this order is attributed to hedgehogs, but there were no hedgehogs in Torran. There is no clear proof that snakes slither along the milky way, but the belief that snakes do indeed engage in an udder business is supported by the writings of the English Bartholomew as far back as the late fourteenth century. Snakes, like hedgehogs and cats, certainly like milk, and unlike tabby's dainty sips, they get stuck in and gulp the milk in great draughts. During the height of the summer feeding, cows often lose milk which snakes are quick to lick. Marks found on the udders of cows were attributed to the roughness of wood, heather and weasels, of which there were plenty in Torran. Those who profess to know about reptilian ways maintain that snakes are incapable of extracting milk from cows. Who knows? Cows can be tetchy creatures and sometimes hold back their milk yield. Whatever the snakes got up to, they did not bite us and the cows on the moorland were far from dry! Indeed, there were occasions when they had to be milked three times a day. Not for nothing did the Saxons call the month of May 'Thrimilce'.

We often saw wild cats on our daily visits to the hens over the hills. Unlike the pine marten which reappeared in Raasay about 1970 after an absence of one hundred years, the wild cat seems to have vanished. Small lizards (*dearcluachrach*) abounded in the mossy swamps and we were warned to keep away from them. Our journey was not complete without a drink from the cool water of the well which had been built many years previously in the shade of the surrounding rock. A very rusty tin can lay on a ledge beside the well and was for the use of passers by. This provision was made at every well by the roadside between Kyle Rona and Brochel Castle. In later years, glass jam jars became fashionable, but the water from the rusty tin refreshed the parts that the jam jar could not reach! The wells, complete with stone hoods, had rising and running water and it was seldom necessary to clean them. The rare weeds in wells and ponds were said to be peculiar to Raasay. During the thirties they were the subject of extensive studies by Professor Harrison and his team, of whom mention has already been made.

The hay and corn were secured by September. Corn took up extensive barn space, and if stored in stacks nearby it enticed mice and rats. The land work involved to secure the corn was considerable. It was taken for granted that fodder was good cattle food, but its nutritional value was low, as minimal seed was left on the stalk. No doubt it was good roughage, but rather an expensive way of manufacturing manure. The hens had a fair share of the seed (oats) and the balance was used for sowing in the following spring. None was sold and the work involved was not justified by the return. Cattle would have been better off with more hay and the poultry would not have starved!

We usually retrieved ears of corn and had fun masking them in foil of various colours, which we had saved from wrapped sweets or biscuits that came our way. The end product looked effective in a vase on the dresser or on the 'room' table.

By the time the autumn equinox caught up, the weather was distinctly autumnal. The leaves and the bracken were fast changing colour. There were still extensive patches of purple heather on the moorland and the odd game-bird had landed in the cookpot. Grouse was not considered to be a choice bird. It was small, tough, and not worth a bullet. No-one believed in letting game hang indefinitely! It was also looked upon as an angry bird from which youngsters should stay clear. The tendency to attack humans was probably attributable to too much testosterone in the body – certainly the case with red grouse – but we did not seek a confrontation.

After school hours we gathered hazel nuts which were around us in profusion and in quick time we were picking brambles by the bucketful. These were never called blackberries. There was a surfeit of ripe wild rosehips which were pleasant to eat. There certainly was no shortage of an intake of vitamin C at this time of year.

It was well into October before the potatoes were lifted. What a tedious job it was! Aunt Mary's hawk-like eyes made sure that we left none in the ground. There was no mechanical equipment, not even a horse-drawn plough to lighten the work. Crofters vied with each other to see who finished first, and who could claim the most potatoes for the winter. Donald Graham seemed to claim more creel-loads than anyone else. Panac proclaimed that he never could count but neighbours took the view that Donald should be good for a touch by the springtime when potatoes were scarce. There was a wonderful crofter community spirit. When we had no potatoes or milk, neighbours supplied some. The milk was usually in bottles which had previously contained whisky. Empty bottles and cans were seldom thrown away. There was always a use for them. When we had milk and a neighbour's cows were farrow, then we returned the compliment. The teacher, who had no croft, was well looked after, and there was no question of money changing hands; but she reciprocated in her own way, usually when the messages arrived from Portree. Money of course was in short supply, but a bartering system without any question of being a repayment did wonders for goodwill.

The potato crop could be anything around fifty creels. The yield in Torran was some seven creels for each creel planted, and as much as possible was secured, usually in a corner of the barn. The remainder was kept in a pit on the croft. It was usual to line the pit with withered dry bracken so as to protect the potatoes from frost. The bracken soon rotted, as did many of the potatoes! It seemed not to have occurred to our elders that a thick layer of earth would have been an easier way, and better for the preservation of the potatoes. It has often occurred to me that in those days crofters made rods for their own backs and created unnecessary work for themselves. I have already made mention of the securing of boats and haymaking. Peat drying was also an unnecessarily protracted process. Fish in quantity was carried from the shore, which was some distance from the houses. They were then promptly beheaded – other than herring – and gutted. The job could have been done by the shore, thus saving time and effort, but for some reason there was an unwritten law that the womenfolk should do this work – a throw-back probably to the days when crowds of island women made for Buckie to gut and cure herring by the shoal.

The nights were lengthening. The cupboard above the stair was full of home-made jam, mostly rhubarb and bramble, but there was also some rowan jelly as a special treat. It was more expensive to make, as apples had to be bought for the purpose, whereas rhubarb and bramble required sugar only to complete the conserve. Despite our strict Presbyterian upbringing, an allowance was made for Hallowe'en. It was probably due to superstition and a belief in the supernatural, which often surfaced as a theme at house ceilidhs. The patronising attitude to tinkers was also a throw-back, as some women still believed that tinker-women had the power of effecting a curse – hence the reason why something, however small, was always bought. I can recall some twenty young people in our own house at Hallowe'en, complete with masks and fancy dress. Everyone had tea and something to eat, but there was no hard drink.

There was a run on in-house games and there were some out-house games also! Old Calum the Brae had his chimney blocked by turf and on another occasion loads of hay were so placed that the window panes were completely covered. The old couple stayed in bed for hours, thinking that it was not yet morning, and only able to live with their memories. It was accepted that some rough treatment might be in store at Hallowe'en and it was taken in good part. Face masks were usually home-made. Tufts of wool and feathers came in useful. Crofters nowadays would think twice about using wool in this way.

Dull November brings the blast,
Then the leaves go whirling past.

There was a mantle of mist on the Stoer and Staffin rocks. The swirling mist was soft and cold but very fresh. It was not to be confused with fog and the smog from which cities, particularly in industrial areas, suffered for decades. We were taught at an early age that if caught in the mist we must stay put and not attempt to head for home. Apart from the hazards that hills and lochs presented, progress by foot would be impeded, and at best, the traveller would end up going round in circles.

We were into winter. During respite from fishing, ewes and wethers were sorted out. Selected animals were slaughtered, some for immediate use and the remainder for the pickling barrel. Uncle Donald was in great demand and he could dispatch a beast in seconds. The method has been illegal for years, with the exception of religious killing such as 'halal'. Uncle Donald could hardly qualify even if he did have Spanish ancestry, which he hotly denied. At about ten years of age we were allowed to watch and indeed to hold the head of the condemned animal at a certain angle, or stir the blood as it poured, then trickled, into the white enamel bucket positioned to receive it. Blood was the main ingredient for black pudding which would be made on the following day. Cattle also were home-killed. Donald Graham was adept at stunning the animal with a quick and firm blow between the horns, administered with a sledge hammer! It was usual for four crofters each to take a share of the slaughtered beast. The meat and offal were divided equally, and by the time we came from school it was all over. We were eating more black pudding (*marag*) in a day or two and enjoying good thick stew made from 'Lady' or 'Nancy', without a murmur. There were no qualms about eating animals that had grown up with us and were part of the crofting scene. Anyway, we knew what we were eating – and it was not a piece of the *each-mart* (cow-horse). The natives of Raasay lived and continue to live with the myth, handed down from generation to generation, that their forbears had been tricked into eating an animal which was part cow and part horse – mongrel meat, so to speak. The word *each-mart* is synonymous to this day with anyone hailing from Raasay. Likewise with fish. Herring was regarded by islanders as the premier fish, surpassing salmon, which few could enjoy. But the folk from Raasay were said to have a better liking for saithe, hence the saying, much slanted for wedding telegrams in times gone by, '*Bu mhath an sgadan an uair nach faighear saoidhean*' – translated: 'herring can be good when no saithe can be got'. Like so many more Gaelic expressions its translation loses effect for those who do not speak the language.

It is believed that the original Gaelic saying referred to the cuddy and not to saithe, the latter being the full-grown fish. In other words, 'a little of what you fancy does you good'. The coal-fish is an intriguing specimen. Unless hooked, it develops through the various stages of cuddy (*cudaig*), podly (*smalag*), saithe (*saoidhean*), large or black saithe (*saoidhean mór no saoidhean dubh*), coal-fish (*ucsa* or *ugsa* – many islanders would use the word '*ucas*'). The fish is good for the table at any of these stages of development, so perhaps the Raasay folk knew more than their Skye kinsfolk about the harvest of the sea!

There was no electricity and no gas, so there were no refrigerators. Most of the meat was pickled, probably the best way of treating cow meat which otherwise could be tough. Personal comfort may have been a consideration, as no-one in my earlier years who had lost their teeth had dentures. People suffered the agony of toothache in order to hold on to their natural teeth, or such as remained of them, as they grew older. It helped to chew salted meat thus tenderised, but the periodic pains from toothache seem not to have been taken into account, even when it upset the immediate convenience of being able to eat in comfort. A carcase of mutton did not last long, and, as it kept very well when hung in an outhouse with good ventilation, most of it was used fresh. A gigot found its way occasionally to favoured relatives in Glasgow. The succulence of mutton from heather-fed animals is *par excellence* and the shop-bought lamb we now have is a poor substitute.

Other than the holly near Aird, the trees – willow, hazel, birch and mountain ash – were bereft of foliage. It was December and there was snow and frost. We spent hours making snowmen and allowed our imagination to run riot in the production of that species. As we grew older and more curious, snow-women followed with distinctive contours. Aunt Mary looked on, in both envy and disbelief, and promptly applied a kettle of hot water to the protrusions. My father's grin suggested that he was satisfied with our healthy approach to creative art.

We were now, and only now, permitted the luxury of warm water for our morning wash, and in consequence, the big cast-iron kettle was in constant demand. The snow did not last long in Raasay but the frosty weather continued for weeks on end. I can recall vividly the crispness of the surroundings, and there have been many occasions since when I have yearned for breaths of such pure and heady air. Christmas was not celebrated officially, although sprigs of holly did find their way to our mantelpiece as we grew older. It was the time of year for a school holiday, and up to 1936 it was preceded by a school treat which was funded out of the teacher's own pocket. After 1936 the treat was not forthcoming, as our teacher at that time related it to Christmas festivities in which she did not believe. The one exception was at the end of 1938 when Donald Maclean was the relief teacher. He 'went to town' and involved one mother from Arnish who certainly did not believe in Christmas but was clearly motivated by Mr Maclean's enthusiasm and leadership. Apart from providing the sandwiches, and very tasty they were, she was full of energy and her sense of fun added to the pleasantries of the occasion. The sound of pipe music attracted Aunt Mary and in quick time she joined the party and helped with the clearing up.

It was the time for the exchange of gifts so the Christmas message must have been somewhere! Relatives from Glasgow and some from Edinburgh sent cakes, fruit, and without fail a large packet of tea. Aunt Mary and Aunt Annie spent much time killing hens and plucking them the following day prior to being parcelled and posted to close relatives. There was a style of procedure to be followed whereby the not-so-close relations got the bird complete with feathers, innards (it would keep better on the way) and an addressed label tied tightly around the neck. The reaction on the receiving end is not known but anyone with some knowledge of life in a town tenement during the mid-thirties can picture the scramble to the dunny and the full use that might have been made of the Corporation wash-houses on these occasions.

There were times too when if the household bedding needed renewing all the birds would be plucked. The feathers were sorted and kept carefully for filling pillows. The stiff feathers from the wings of the birds in demise were made into a *badag* (brush) and often used for the removal of burnt oatmeal from the griddle when baking oatcakes. Whatever the method of bird dispatch – parcelled or complete with feathers – the postal service delivered the goods, fresh and wholesome. The system was trusted completely. One would hesitate these days to send fresh produce even by first-class mail.

We always looked forward to New Year. The young men from Fladda, Torran, Arnish and Brochel Castle engaged in some 'first footing'. Visitors were made doubly welcome, especially if they proffered a dram. The woman of the house produced the glasses which were small and did not permit the addition of water. Adding water to whisky was simply not done. She only had to taste the stuff and it went promptly 'to her head' – perhaps a small matter of proof! Sore heads or not, everyone was in their place by midday on New Year's Day for the church service, dependent on a minister or lay preacher being available. It was not unknown for some young men to produce a dram discreetly within the precincts of the church. It follows that spirits and the Bible – usually the New Testament, as it took up less space – shared the inside pocket of the Sunday suit on this annual occasion. It was a change from peppermints.

CHAPTER 3

LIFE AT SCHOOL

I went to school at the prescribed age of five, proudly sporting a new pair of short trousers made by Mrs Cumming, Kyle Rona, from her father's tweed coat. He was by then an old man and would not be needing it. She was the possessor of a marvellous invention – a hand-operated Singer sewing machine. Mrs Cumming could not sing, but that is by the way. No-one else produced such machines and any that may still be around could fetch a good penny. Peggy-Bella, then about fourteen years old and the oldest of the Cumming daughters, of whom there were five, came specially to Torran on a wet July evening, to hand over this garment, proudly letting it be known that she had finished it off with some of her very own hand sewing.

The Cumming family lived in Kyle Rona, some three long and hard-going miles from Torran. Miles still to this day seem longer in the Highlands of Scotland. They had lived previously in Eilean Tigh (Island of One House). This island was a mere piece of rock with one house nestling under a promontory. There was little earth, far less vegetation. Here, however, had lived Seonnaidh Mor (big John), the father of Mrs Cumming and many others. He was also one of my own great-uncles. Apart from having been known in his day as a very strong man who could lift a boll of meal with his teeth, he was a good seaman and no mean bard (poet). His Gaelic compositions were not, unfortunately, recorded! With a few exceptions they are lost to posterity.

What a pity that tape recorders were not available in those days and that there was such reluctance to convey words to paper. The latter was often due to sheer pride as it would in many cases mean enlisting the help of someone who had been taught to write.

It is interesting to find that whilst English was neither spoken nor written, there were those from a generation long since gone who could write in Gaelic. They were self-taught simply by following the twice-daily Bible-reading in Gaelic that took place in every home. There were no doubt weaknesses in spelling but most could read in Gaelic. One poignant poem by Seonnaidh Mor, overflowing with sadness, dealt with the Highland Clearances. An inadequate translation of the chorus captures something of the melancholia which prevailed at a time when relations and neighbours were about to leave for foreign shores, by order of their landlord:

> My heart is sad, my heart is sad
> This cause for sadness how can it be;
> I'm low in spirit, there is no uplift
> As we set sails to leave Portree.

School was an agreeable part of my formative years. There was no prescribed school uniform but most of the boys wore corduroy short trousers, dark blue woollen jerseys, woollen stockings with turnovers and tackety boots. The girls had greater sartorial freedom but in my earlier school days they all wore high laced boots and long woollen stockings which covered their knees. They were privileged to have black nugget for polishing their footwear, but the boys had to make do with dubbin – a kind of sweet-smelling grease. At least it kept the leather supple. Shoes were for the Sabbath when movement and noise were expected to be minimal. They were strictly for the church services part of the Sabbath, and, like one's best clothes, had to give way to the work-a-day articles once the last service was over and the privacy of the household had been gained once more.

Patched trousers and darned stockings were common sights. The results were both works of art and necessity and we were brought up to appreciate thrift. No household sewing kit was complete without at least one darning needle.

> Don't be ashamed of a patch, dear –
> A patch is not anything base –
> A patch is a strip of honour
> That never can bring disgrace.

I reflected on this jingle in later years on seeing Lord Longford – more than once – with elbow patches on his jacket. It could have been the same jacket year in, year out! The patches could also have been for extra protection or, like Benn's beverage beaker, a symbol of the brotherhood of man. The patches were real enough, but whether or not they covered the real wear and tear of 'elbow grease' was not established! In Torran, they certainly covered our basic needs and a patch, contrary to the rhyme, was something base in the literal sense.

My first teacher, Miss Campbell, affectionately known to us as Rita, but never addressed as such in class, came from Scullamus, near Broadford, Skye. She was a disciplinarian, but what a teacher! She had taken over from Seumas Ruadh (Ginger James) who was very crippled and could only get about with the aid of a stick. School lessons had been mostly in Gaelic, the native tongue. He must truly have been the forerunner of liberal studies. The children certainly had the benefit of an unfettered outdoor life, and when the older boys felt that there was a tightening up of school discipline, for some mysterious reason the chimney began to have 'blowdowns', and this always heralded the end of another school day. One day a boy slipped off the slate roof when

93

placing turf over the chimney pot, and that prank came to a speedy and not very dignified end.

The seat of the schoolmaster's wooden chair was circular and for some unknown reason there was a small hole right through the middle. On some occasions the poor man, who took much for granted, had the discomfort of sitting with some force on to the sharp end of a slate pencil. Why the hole was not sealed off always remained a mystery but it was on such occasions that a modicum of short-lived discipline was applied by Ginger James. Before taking up a teaching post he had been a Customs and Excise Officer but he seemed to have forgotten long ago where his duty lay! Imagine Rita's shock to find that children at the age of ten and over, including my oldest brother, had the barest knowledge of the English language. Her task was a formidable one but she could claim to have won the day. People who have achieved less have been awarded medals.

The school seats with desk tops could accommodate five children comfortably. The teacher's own desk was a massive piece of carpentry, and the inside housed materials such as chalk, textbooks with answers section and the tawse, the leather all the way from Lochgelly.

The school blackboard was also large, standing in a varnished wooden frame with two legs and cross pieces of wood for feet, similarly treated. It was not known ever to have fallen over so it must have been well balanced in construction. The board was subjected to considerable chalk abuse and it was the teacher's job to apply a fresh coat of special black paint at the end of term. The National Union of Teachers had yet to be born!

A large map of the world with the British Empire highlighted in pink, maps of the British Isles and the continents, a calendar, a chart showing the flags in colour that make up the Union Jack and a Union Jack flag, adorned the walls. A big swivelled globe of the world had pride of place on one of the window ledges. There were no visual aids, such as may be seen on the walls of modern day schools, and the budget did not run to flip charts.

The school in Torran with its fourteen scholars – they were never referred to as pupils, not even by the teacher – was a mere few yards away from our own house. We had a black and white collie called Lassie, and within minutes of four o'clock, when the schoolday finished, she could be heard giving a strange whine. Indeed, our teacher, often engrossed in her work and certainly not a clock watcher, needed no further reminding that our day was done. By the time we bounded out, Lassie was welcoming us with her own special 'bow-wow' tune, at the school garden gate. She was hopeless as a sheepdog but had great perception, was as soft as butter and just loved children. She pawed us and licked us. We were told not to let cats breathe over us for fear of asthma, but dogs could lick us to their hearts' content because their tongue-licking could heal our cuts! This old folk's tale, and a dangerous one it is, persists in country places to this day. We knew nothing about conveyable diseases such as liver infection.

The school building in Torran had two porches, one for the boys and one for the girls. Nowadays, they would be called cloakrooms. The dry closets, the use of which was not encouraged, were in an outside projection to the back of the school and carried no sign to discriminate sex. Who can fathom the working of educational minds by the latter quarter of the nineteenth century when the school was built? The porches were obvious gathering places for the children in inclement weather. By the time that I went to school, numbers had dwindled and the front porch only was in use. Peggy, a girl from Arnish, in her fourteenth year, had found the new teaching methods which Rita had introduced a bit too much for her, and one of my earliest school recollections of these porch morning gatherings was hearing her tell my brother that she so wished she was a hen. As I thought of all the extra eggs that could be sold in Portree, the school whistle went – Rita never used the school bell – and poor Peggy had to face yet another day wrestling with the 'three Rs'.

I was born left-handed. Any ideas I may have harboured about writing with my left hand were soon dispelled and a few cracks on the knuckles with a ruler corrected the defect! It may or may not have affected my nervous disposition: I do not know, but I can lay claim to ambidextrous activities over the years!

Charles Mackenzie, one of the oldest of the boys in school at that time, on receiving a slap for his carelessness retaliated by giving the teacher one back. He was kept in for a whole hour after class. With a long three-mile walk back to Brochel Castle where he lived, this was punishment indeed, more so as the evening shadows fell early and the weather was wet. The experience was at least relieved with a tasty sandwich given to him by his teacher when she sent him on his way! Justice was seen to be done by the punishment inflicted. The school incident was forgotten quickly and Charles developed a healthy respect for his teacher. Nowadays, he would probably have ended up in a remand centre whilst the teacher would be crucified by the anti-corporal punishment brigade. Charles left school, as every pupil did, at the age of fourteen, and gave a lifetime of service to the police, during which time no doubt he had occasion to recall his personal experience when dealing with cases of assault.

School attendance was anything but comfortable for Peggy-Bella and her sisters who had to traverse on foot miles of very rough track, five days a week. They often arrived wet but seldom late, and the teacher dried their clothes in front of a blazing coal fire. The age of plastics was still a long way off. There were no radiators. There was no boiler house.

There were no school meals either, but in the depths of winter the education authority provided one jar of Horlicks malted milk, priced at eight shillings and sixpence – so it was a large jar. There was also some cocoa which I suspected was often subsidised by our kindly teachers over the years. School started at ten o'clock and finished at four o'clock. The Cumming girls waited patiently at the red gate above our own house until my sister and I, under the firm direction of Aunt Mary, turned up with cooked salt herring and boiled jacket potatoes. This was their daily 'fish and chips' – what a treat for hungry girls on a long trek at the end of school days! As time went by school numbers dwindled, and like the ten green bottles, by 1938 Betsy, the youngest of the Cumming school girls, was the sole beneficiary of the tattie and herring bounty.

It is remarkable how, over the years, the common fare of the islanders has found new status. In London, Glasgow and other places where Highlanders and islanders gather, tattie and herring suppers are scrumptious affairs – not to mention sumptuous. Cakes have a low rating whenever home-made scones, pancakes and potato scones are on the bill of fare.

Rita owned a gramophone, complete with winding handle. At the end of singing lessons, when full use was made of the tuning fork, we had the novel experience of listening to recorded songs by singers such as Neil Maclean and Archie Grant. Nothing however must be taken for granted. On one occasion at the start of a gramophone session, when I was only months at school, excitement got the better of me and I clapped. The gramophone was turned off and I was in disgrace for days. Next time my emotions were much better controlled! Talk of lessons in self-discipline! Looking back it all seemed so infantile but Rita took over a school in disarray and felt that points of discipline had to be made for the immediate benefit of the teacher and the long-term benefit of the pupils. She was absolutely right. Her 'scholars' have lived full lives enriched by her philosophy. Dancing-steps, to the horror of one housewife in Arnish, were introduced with the help of accordion music on records together with a melodeon which Rita also possessed. This innovation was listed conveniently as part of physical exercises, known to us as 'drill'. Boys and girls were put through their paces, with shoulders well back as a basic rule – stand at ease; stand erect; to numbers (1 to 8); hands on shoulders; upwards stretch; hands on shoulders; forward stretch; hands on shoulders; sideways stretch; hands on shoulders; hands down; legs across sit – and again to numbers in that position; knees bend to floor and up; touch your toes – all first-class stuff, and we were as supple as willow twigs. Cousin Alick's trousers, hanging on one button only at the back, gave way during a 'touch your toes' exercise. It was hands to trousers as an additional exercise for him, but we dared not acknowledge his predicament which also had not escaped our teacher. All the lads from then on made sure that the button-holes in their braces were occupied by buttons. Belts came into fashion much later, at least in Torran.

The two minutes' silence at eleven o'clock on the eleventh of November each year in commemoration of those who fell in the Great War – Armistice day – is a memory that has stayed with me over the years. Torran was a quiet place at any time, but during these two minutes we barely breathed; a pin would not dare drop and it seemed as if the beasts of the field and the fowls of the air also took note of the annual token of respect for the fallen. The observance over the years of this period of silence, reflected in the gatherings at cenotaphs, seemed not to compare with the depth of silence experienced at school. Was it an unduly deep school discipline – a sensitivity on my part and surely not on my part alone? It left its impressions and cannot be explained away.

Rita moved on during my fourth year at school and we lost a first-class teacher. She took up a teaching post in

Sconser, Skye. It was short-lived and she was soon back to Torran, but this time as the bride of James Graham who made a lifetime career in the lighthouse service.

Miss Macdonald, from Elgol, Skye, affectionately known to us as Nellie, was my next teacher in Torran. She too was brilliant, possessing her own individual style which permitted us to relax occasionally in class. She was a marvellous developer of character but did not overlook what she considered as the effectiveness of the strap! I was once at the receiving end for not remembering the number of spans in the Forth Bridge. I always check that they are still there when in the area! Although we worked hard in school, there was a good deal of homework, including committing to memory most of the psalms in metre, a few 'approved' paraphrases such as 'O God of Bethel', but only one or two hymns as these 'were not the inspired word of God' – so said the lady from the Brae, in her protest to the teacher. However, we learnt all about 'Cool Siloam's shady rill' and Nelly got away with it as an exercise in singing. There was no parents' committee but little escaped at least one self-righteous watchdog.

We also had to commit to memory the Shorter Catechism – all 107 questions and answers. Starting with the Decalogue, the Creed was also included, but the correct meaning of the word 'catholic' was emphasised. We were not asked to memorise 'Grace before Meat' and 'Grace after Meat' as these bordered on prescribed prayers – forbidden Episcopalian habits! Following on the heels of all this came Scripture prose – 'Ho everyone that thirsteth' – Isaiah Chapter 55 (all of it) comes to mind, simply because cousin Alick, of slipped trousers fame, once asked the teacher to be excused for a drink of water.

Writers not inspired by the 'Word' were not overlooked! There were long pieces from Shakespeare's *The Merchant of Venice* and *As You Like It*. The contribution of poets such as

Wordsworth – 'The Daffodils' and innumerable sonnets; Cowper, Shelley, Byron, Longfellow – *Hiawatha*; Keats – 'Ode to a Nightingale' and other odes; Milton – 'When I consider how my life is spent' (we hoped that we were only on the threshold of ours) was studied. Works by Sir Walter Scott – *The Lady of the Lake* and *The Lay of the Last Minstrel* – were included for good measure. The poems of Walter De La Mare were popular and I enjoyed reciting 'Abou Ben Adhem', one of James Leigh Hunt's best known poems. Another favourite, by Thomas Hood, was 'I Remember', which incidentally was the subject of a question on the television programme *Mastermind* in 1984.

Exercises in arithmetic were completed on slates, and the new chalk slim-line 'pencils' were much preferred to the hard slate pencils with the incessant scratching, no doubt induced by the users! The correction of arithmetic was carried out by class members on a subtle system of slate exchange, relieving the teacher of at least one chore. No-one cheated. English grammar and literature were well taught. Text-books were pictorial and were mostly 'Blackie's' or 'Collins'' and a fair selection was kept in the large glass-fronted double bookcase donated by James Coates to many such schools. His name was inscribed boldly on a plaque fixed to the front of the rather ornate portable top of the bookcase. We were soon to learn all about James Coates the philanthopist and owner of textile mills in Paisley. Gaelic lessons were given twice weekly. As it was the native tongue, these lessons, including Gaelic recitation and the full use of Macalpine's Gaelic and English Dictionary, now a prized possession, gave us some appreciation of the beauty and depth of the language.

Dictation put us on the spot and our spelling caught us out. Transcription was monotonous but at least it was straightforward. Composition was a favourite subject. It developed our thinking but its appeal was simply because we could use our imagination. Sheila Cumming let hers run riot. A common subject was an imaginary autobiography. When it was the turn of the frog, Sheila finished off by writing that she jumped into a pail of hot water and was burnt to death. Perhaps she should have turned into a prince and lived in France to croak the tale! She lost marks on perception.

The director of education for Inverness-shire, Murdo Morrison, a Lewis man, who even then seemed to us to be quite old, visited Torran school periodically, as did HM Inspectors of Schools. Mr Morrison was informal and kind but he did not miss a trick. I am convinced that he knew that our teacher, who stood behind him, was giving us silent clues to help us with our answers to his questions. Why else did he perch himself on the top of a front desk when he could have stood, done a 'Mastermind' or, for that matter, sat wherever he chose? He lived, deservedly, to a great age.

On the subject of outdoor pastimes, cousin John and I were in the front line when it came to 'do and dare'. One of John's favourite activities was to hop along the school garden wall, which was stone-built, and jump from one gatepost to another across a rather wide gate with sturdy metal bars which criss-crossed. He was out to impress Sheila Cumming, with whom he sat in school, and for whom, even at such tender years, he had some reciprocated affection. One wet morning, as the school bell shrilled its clarion call, John missed the gatepost and he too has a leg scar as a legacy. Sheila, bless her, promptly reported herself present and then told the teacher of the incident. The Lord's Prayer was recited rather quickly and then it was time to see to John! The teacher did a professional job of the dressing. It was promptly followed by a dressing down, and I, who had stood by him, was peremptorily instructed to accompany him home. I duly returned to my classes and felt a sense of injustice on finding myself marked absent in the register for the forenoon session. Such was school justice! Another of our pranks was to run over the flat top of a hill above Uncle Donald's house (Am Meall) and jump over it backwards, righting ourselves in space before landing on, fortunately for our own preservation, a soft patch below. John's oldest brother, Murdo, on discovering what we were up to, soon put a stop to our foolhardiness with a threat of 'I'll tell father'.

As our schooling developed so did our taste for competitions. Next to the *Bulletin* (long since demised), the favourite paper was the *People's Journal*, all the way from Dundee. I took the initiative and sent off my answers to a relatively simple competition in the 'Sadie Sunshine' column, accompanied by a photograph of Murdo my brother, Janet my sister and myself. Imagine our surprise and delight when a box of assorted chocolates arrived as a prize! Aunt Mary and my father had some nagging doubts that it may not have been a prize; if indeed it was bought, where had the money come from? It was most hurtful to be so closely questioned and under suspicion of malpractice. Our family picture, with due reference, splashed on a page of the *People's Journal* finally convinced them and my rating went up tremendously. Next day, during the geography lesson, came the inquisition about the Forth Bridge – a 'set-up' job I am sure! I also mixed up the stations on the LMS and LNER lines, and for these failures I received two strokes of the four-fingered strap. It was a good job that Miss Nelly did not award strokes for each span and station! Anyway, I felt well and truly put in my place, more so as I knew she had already seen the prized *People's Journal*. Her defensive mechanism simply went into action: no pupil could be permitted to develop big ideas. Years later, in 1964 in fact, we travelled on the same coach from Skye to Glasgow and had tea in Tyndrum. She told me that she always recalled my ability with mental arithmetic. What a revelation, twenty-eight years on! She also told me that on the same coach was an old lady who had been her own teacher. She still looked sprightly, and my great regret was that neither of us had a camera to capture the three generations of 'teachers and taught'.

Nelly moved on to another teaching post after a mere two school terms in Torran where she was greatly respected. She was succeeded by another Miss Macdonald, from Ullapool. She had traversed Canada and was, to say the least, eccentric, especially at full-moon time. She arrived in Torran with a great load of furniture, which my brother, cousins and I – then aged eleven – helped to carry up the steep brae from that part of the rocky shore known to us as Laimrig a Leodhasaich (the Lewisman's 'Landing'). There must have been a long-forgotten story attached to that name somewhere. She was accompanied by her father and stepmother, the latter looking no older than her stepdaughter. Although forty-six years old at that time, our teacher-to-be was seen to burst into tears saying that she was homesick. 'How can such a thing be,' said her father, 'you have been as far away as Vancouver and in other exciting places such as Abhainnsuidh, not to mention Ardamhoorlidh' (in far away Harris where lived a youngster called 'Finlay J' – later to become a producer of programmes on radio, and a writer). She cried on.

Her stepmother was a charming soul who accepted the situation with a good grace. Miss Macdonald did not take kindly to her stepmother, so goodness knows what she said about her before and after meals! One of our new teacher's innovations was to dispose of the school strap. Our initial reaction was one of pleasure, but it was short lived. Rumour reached us, much later, that she had been in trouble for using the strap indiscriminately in a previous school in Harris. She certainly had the ability to teach but her own state of mind from time to time left her pupils tense and unhappy. Children have great powers of discernment and we could tell her moods like the tides. When she was in fine form, her well kept grey hair was combed above her ears ending up in the then fashionable bun well up to the back of her head. When she was anything but in good form, her hair came down over her ears and the bun was at a much lower level, virtually ending up over the back of her high-necked dress. What psychologists could make of this diagnosis of temperament I do not know, nor much care, but as sure as God made little apples, the modes of hair dressing which I have described certainly coincided with her moods.

Another strange phenomenon was her pose. When 'not herself', she stood sideways facing the windows, which other than a double window near the high ceiling to the rear of the building, were on one wall only, at right angles to the classroom seating arrangement, and addressed her class in that posture. She worked from a table – never from the large sloping-top desk so thoughtfully provided for teachers who might be tempted to nod off behind the screen which the desk slope provided. She was seldom seen to sit down, even at her work table. All our teachers were good writers but she was supreme. We were taught the rule of the pen with lean strokes up and fat strokes down:

> The Pickwick, the Owl and the Waverley Pen
> Came as a boon and a blessing to Men.

What a pity that Biro pens were ever discovered!

Her teaching of English grammar was unique. Parsing, particular and general analysis were hammered home but we enjoyed the experience of being nailed down! The lessons left lasting impressions, if only a continuing awareness of shortcomings when dealing with split infinitives and parts of the verb 'to be'.

She made periodic jaunts, always on the evening of a school day, to the shop at Millplace in the south end of

Raasay and about fifteen miles from Torran. This meant a return walk from the schoolhouse at Brochel Castle. She was picked up by Ewen Macrae in his solid black Austin car at Brochel, and of course, after her shopping spree and a welcome late high tea with the Macraes, the return car journey to Brochel was completed. On one such occasion she invited me to accompany her. To me, it was a convenient royal command, as a visit to the shop was a rare treat. Aunt Mary was only too happy to acquiesce. My sister and cousin Chrissie had mixed feelings, as they were rather wary of Miss Macdonald's moods. It was late autumn and our walk to Brochel was brisk and pleasant. She was received like a lady by 'J.B.', the owner of the shop – a valued customer who bought well, and, more importantly, paid cash on the spot.

He soon established who I was, even though when he asked me 'who do you belong to?' I replied cryptically 'to my father'. He was not known for his good moods when dealing with customers but I got 'the treatment' and left the shop with a free and sizeable poke of peppermints. Some time later, after our family moved to the south end of Raasay, I made frequent visits to the shop and found 'J.B.' (another John Nicolson) a most charming person, other than on such occasions as when Ibbag, a local old maid who used me as a runner for bogie roll which she smoked, and quite often chewed, was looking for tick!

'J.B.' was a native of Raasay who, as a young lad, had left home to follow a career in commerce. For some three decades he was connected with the biscuit business and lived in Whitley Bay, the home of many an exiled Scot. But his native island was calling and he returned to Raasay in the early thirties, to follow in his father's footsteps as the local grocer. His two shop assistants for the following years, Ronnie and Donnie, were well trained by 'J.B.'. They knew exactly the level of stock needed to keep their customers happy in all seasons, at the same time avoiding unnecessary capital outlay, thereby protecting what is now called cash flow!

But I have digressed. On our walk back from Brochel, Miss Macdonald criticised me strongly for using the word 'was' other than when in the indicative mood, during part of our conversation. It was raining heavily by this time and I was carrying one of her bags of messages which was anything but light. I can still hear her prattling on about parts of the verb 'to be' and indeed see her in my mind's eye as Torran came in sight at the top of Tairbort. I could gladly have seen her wet bag of groceries burst into the water-logged ditch at the side of the stony path. She clouded over for me an otherwise pleasant evening but I did not spurn the proffered half-crown as she wished me goodnight. At that moment I felt that my hurt pride would give way gracefully to such considerations of vast wealth. I said nothing to Aunt Mary about the lesson in grammar on the moors of Arnish. Anyway, she would not have understood. The following evening, after homework was completed, much time was occupied perusing the ever popular catalogues of Smart and B. G. May! Sometime later I was to obtain a deeper inkling, if not complete understanding, of my teacher's concern for the correct use of grammar. She had encouraged me to take what was then known as the Bursary Examination. I completed the questions paper on a warm May day in Raasay School where the invigilator was Ewen Macrae. Like the local shoemaker, he held a number of roles in the community, and as representative or agent for Baird and Company, who owned the mineral rights near the pier and a large slice of real estate, he was privileged to live in a big house in its own lush grounds and could certainly claim one-upmanship over the shoemaker who also represented real estate owned by the Department of Agriculture for Scotland. I do not know what qualities Mr Macrae possessed to become an invigilator for school examinations, but he made sure that the blotters were clean and that the pockets of candidates were not within easy reach. I did not find the questions too taxing even if one of my answers was veiled in allegory, and I confused being distinguished with being extinguished in one of the translations.

In due course, a letter from the director of education, addressed to myself and not to my parent, informed me that I 'had not obtained the requisite number of marks'. I have always remembered the wording. My father maintained, and his theory may well have been correct, that the reply to the pre-examination questionnaire, which he as a parent was required to complete, was the governing factor in deciding whether or not a pupil would be awarded a bursary. A statement of parent's income was viewed with misgiving and perhaps concern when the income was virtually nil. The education authority might well have felt that even a reasonably bright pupil could turn out to be a financial embarrassment to the establishment, if a relatively small bursary was all that was available. Winners of these bursaries transferred to Portree school for higher education and the cost of staying in the school hostel was a substantial part of the overheads which parents were expected to meet. My father was perhaps too honest in his submissions! Transfer to Portree High School is now an automatic process for school children in Raasay and other island areas, and although there is an expense for parents, the system offers far more to pupils than was the case when I was twelve years of age. The failure to pass the examination left me somewhat mortified, more so as my teacher, Miss Macdonald, had given up the Easter vacation in order to give me additional coaching. It was a generous gesture and her reaction when I did not make the grade was equally generous. She made the point that this was what examinations were for – some succeed, some do not – but the look in her eye said a good deal more.

It was Miss Macdonald at her best, and I am sure that the thought of 'a feather in her own cap', had I been successful, was well down her scale of values at that moment. Her standard of professional ethics and loyalty to the educational system could not permit her to develop the theme further when, later on, she and my father were in analytical discourse.

School life still had its moments of comedy. Our teacher had borrowed our cat, Daisy, to keep an eye on mice which she asserted had virtually taken over the classroom. One late afternoon when she was particularly edgy and had concluded that all the set school tasks had been met for that day, she decided to engage in loud reading of portions of *The Pilgrim's Progress*. She was somewhere in the Slough of Despond when she gave a loud scream, threw the book towards the class and called on my cousin Chrissie to come and remove the mouse which, she said, had gone up her clothes. Chrissie having dutifully obeyed the summons, simply stood still beside her distraught teacher. 'Chrissie, do something', whereupon Chrissie touched the edge of the teacher's skirt. 'Don't do that – don't do that – get back to your seat at once.' Barely had this been said and as quickly acted upon than it was followed with 'all stand and repeat the Lord's Prayer'. We obeyed, panfaced and dutifully and were then dismissed some thirty minutes ahead of the normal time schedule. The incident was logged in the school register. Our search for mice to provide a repeat performance was in vain.

During these periods of strange moods we certainly had exercises in mental stress. She would, in her darkest moods, split the school into Nicolson and Macleod groups. The outsider, Betsy Cumming, was used to even the number! One or other, but not both groups simultaneously, were 'in the doghouse' on such occasions. After morning recital of the Lord's Prayer, she would ask those 'in disgrace' to remain standing and then in an imperious voice demand to know:

'Is the Nicolson Clan settled today?' We replied, far more shakily than if she had used the tawse on us: 'Yes'. This question and response were always in Gaelic! On one occasion cousin Chrissie was accused of sniggering the answer and for this crime she had to stand on a chair behind the class for the rest of the morning, whilst the teacher baked pancakes for the Macleods who, that day, were in favour. Chrissie's father, Uncle Donald, not one to mince his words, called at the school after hours and gave Miss Macdonald a verbal lashing, even threatening, if ever there was a repeat performance, to put her, like the washing, under plenty of stones in the brook near by! This was exciting stuff which we could hear so clearly from our own house. There was no school next day and the policeman arrived – a rare event indeed – all the way from Portree. Matters went no further. He had tea on neutral ground – our house – and we enjoyed his sweets. Miss Macdonald changed her tune abruptly and reverted to educating us.

Some days later, Uncle Donald received by post two ounces of his favourite tobacco, from an anonymous source. Later on in the week we saw him leave fresh fish and potatoes on the schoolhouse doorstep! His family pew was immediately in front of the teacher's pew and according to Bellag Handy, they exchanged imperials on the following Sabbath! Torran had no need of a parents and teachers association.

Miss Macdonald believed in keeping us informed about world events. Monday, Wednesday and Friday were post-delivery days. Armed with two copies of the *Bulletin*, then the most popular newspaper in the Highlands, she would, with commentary, go through each page in order of date, systematically, with the pupils gathered round her so that they could all see the pictures. Mussolini and Hitler were in the news increasingly but what sticks mostly in my mind was the sensation caused by the abdication of King Edward

VIII. Wallis Warfield Simpson was denigrated and quite unsuitable as Queen Consort. The human failing of the uncrowned king tended to be glossed over and Mrs Simpson – described by 'Panac' as 'that woman of sin, with the flat chest' – was the cause of all the trouble.

We were brought up to believe in royalty and the establishment with all their fripperies. The church and the school preached and taught us that a crowned head of state was divinely appointed. We saw it in the insular context of Great Britain with an empire and dominions which on the map of the world and the globe showed massive chunks in red over the face of the earth. The French ate frogs and were an evil lot who had guillotined their king and queen. The Union of Soviet and Socialist Republics was dismissed out of hand as atheistic. America had Hollywood, Chicago and gangsters – and a President – but Roosevelt found favour. We understood Americans to be pro-British and white. Our education somehow did not take note of the Deep South other than some reference to slave trading – a most unfortunate occurrence in American history – which, like the American Civil War, was best forgotten.

Still, there was a lack of logic somewhere. Our history lessons covered the British Civil War in great detail. Charles I was the villain of the piece and Cromwell was placed on a pedestal of near sainthood. Could the approach and thinking conceivably have been moulded round the part played by the Covenanters in those days?

These days were long gone. The abdication of Edward VIII was news. It upset convention but within months there was a coronation and the 'Ship of State' was soon back on an even keel. We lived for the present in Torran school and as a special treat we had the continuing cartoon strip of Potter! When Potter was passed over, we knew that one of Miss Macdonald's dreaded moods was upon us. She had a pleasing voice and we had many psalm-singing lessons.

Songs were taboo but for some reason she made two exceptions; 'An t-Eilean Muileach' and 'Am Bothan Beag' (The Isle of Mull and the Wee Bothy). Listening to them being sung, after all these years, brings back schoolday memories. I was in good voice as a schoolboy and when it broke at a youngish age, our teacher was much displeased and said it was my own fault for carrying too much peat on my back! What Miss Macdonald really needed was a man. Some said that she had been jilted and that was the reason for her going off to Vancouver. Who can say! Faith is all very well but a bit of love-life makes our short stay on earth much more agreeable – and who can suggest a better hobby!

When I left Raasay for my first job assignment and not yet sixteen, she gave me a reference. It was written beautifully on paper of parchment quality and the phraseology included the words: 'he has understanding and perception much in advance of his years'. I took her word for it – so did my future employers! Alexandrina Macdonald came to love Raasay. She retired to Inverarish where for a few years she disturbed her immediate neighbours by her antics and, like the weather, provided a talking point. She lived on in her own strange ways and kept her assignment with the 'Grim Reaper' in her early seventies.

Two other teachers carried out relief duties during spells of medical leave for Miss Macdonald. The first was Donald Maclean from Locheport, North Uist, who some years later took up a teaching post in Staffin, Skye, from where, on the steep rugged coastline, there is an excellent view of the north end of Raasay, Fladda and Rona. He fascinated us with his great interest in weather forecasting, a project incidentally to which he applied his perceptive talents over the following decades. He collated a priceless record of detail, which is now available as a booklet, 'Weather in North Skye'. Apart from providing a running record of the weather it also contains an interesting historical slant on temperamental

111

climatic variations. Rainfall comparisons and temperature of the atmosphere have appeared frequently in local newspapers and the information imparted is followed assiduously by many readers, not simply confined to the islands and the Highlands of Scotland. He retired from teaching in 1972 after forty-three years' service and continued to live in Skye.

During his time in Torran we were regaled with violin and bagpipe music. Not since the days of our beloved Rita did we have such a treat. Some locals did not approve but his personality won the day. Many years later he gave of his musical talents freely at a concert in Portree, arranged through myself on behalf of the Gaelic Society of London, for the Fund in aid of the Highlands and Islands Eventide Homes, set up by the Society in 1965.

Donald Maclean never used corporal punishment in Torran school and I would be surprised if he used it in any other school either. He had a wonderful way with children and we benefited from his teaching. Physical exercises were linked up with sport, and shinty had a new identity as distinct from the mongrel game of shinty and hockey combined, to which we had become accustomed! Learning was a pleasure and we enjoyed going to school. The days went by too quickly and instead of longing for four o'clock when school dismissed, we found ourselves fighting the clock to complete projects. He was a great believer in delegation and whatever we did by way of school work was spiced with challenge and interest. He was blessed with an even temper and I do not recall seeing him ruffled at any time. To be fair to ourselves, we appreciated the new style of discipline and did our best to give satisfaction. It was a wonderful team spirit and I have reflected on this happy era of schooling many times during adult life. Creative art, liberal studies or social skills and the use of leisure-time were ingredients of a teaching philosophy, the art of which he knew how to apply.

The second teacher was a rather young lady from Valtos

in Skye. Grammar was one of her favourite subjects and we spent some time comparing newspaper editorials. She considered the style of presentation in the *Daily Express* to be poor but viewed that in the *Manchester Guardian* with approbation. Her reaction to the lack of literary style in most newspapers today would be interesting. I sensed that she was politically 'left of centre' but other than discussing politics in the course of history lessons, all our teachers were careful not to show political bias. During this period, our lessons in algebra and geometry were infrequent and in our short-term way of thinking, we were very happy with the arrangement!

I was in my fourteenth year when we moved to Oscaig, in May 1939. We were now in the south end of Raasay and had to attend another school. Raasay school was, to my sister and myself, a big school. The kindly Miss Tallach was headmistress but the scene was dominated by Mr Malcolm Gillies, the school master who took the senior classes. 'Blackie', as he was known, was not backward in administering the hard feel of a pointer or the odd ear pull! He was regarded as a terror, a reputation which had followed him from a previous teaching post, but I would like to think that he also commanded respect. I certainly respected him. After due deliberation he considered that I could hold my place in the most senior class – Advanced Division II. I was well tested by him over a few days in advance and the thought that I just might be relegated to Advanced Division I, with only a few more school months left between me and the freedom to leave school, caused me some anguish but spurred me on to give of my very best.

The school-leaving age at that time was fourteen. It was of course possible to carry on with further education in Portree. This was based on passing a bursary examination around the age of twelve and was, as I have already suggested, probably a means test for parents, with their ability

113

to meet costs a major consideration, bearing in mind that the bursary award was quite small. The system seemed grossly unfair, as pupils with homes near Portree had a distinct advantage over those in places further afield such as certain areas in Skye, Harris and North Uist. Despite such constraints these areas produced many distinguished scholars and Raasay was well represented. The Macleans, known locally as 'the tailor's family', were the best known in my own generation. Their literary contributions live on. Sons and daughters of Raasay have over many years contributed to medicine, law, arts and sciences. Mr Macleod, the shoemaker already referred to, and his wonderful wife, Lexy, did their best for their family's education and they were not to be disappointed. There was little money in shoe-repairing or indeed in any of the other jobs which came the shoemaker's way, and further education for a large family must have strained the household resources to the very limit. Despite all these self-imposed trials there was the will and the ability to exchange pleasantries and show hospitality to all comers.

Raasay school is over one mile from Oscaig, much further away than the Torran school was from our home there. Aunt Mary provided us with a 'piece' for our lunch break. When the school reopened in August, my sister was provided with lunch at Uncle John's house in Inverarish. Uncle John was a kind man but rather grumpy and it was his daughter Mary-Anne who really made the arrangements. There was no word about my needs – I was overlooked completely – so much for equality of the sexes! Anyway, I continued to enjoy my buttered oatcakes and scones with rhubarb jam in the company of mischievous youngsters, in the nicest way, such as Brisco, Calum Ban and 'Captain Brown'. They came from places even further away than Oscaig – Eyre and East Suishnish.

Prunella Stack in her book *Island Quest* tells us that

Murdo Nicolson, the late author's brother, doubtlessly absorbed in scripture (early 1960s)

The author's wedding, 27 December 1949. Picture taken on the lounge of the Portree Hotel on the Isle of Skye minutes before the memorable boat trip to the reception at the Raasay Hotel. From left to right: the author's cousin Torquil (who later married Mary Ann, sister of the author's wife), the author, the author's wife, Catriona, Neilana (Catriona's sister) and Jessie (the author's sister), affectionately known as Janet.

The author's wife, Catriona, as a young girl (1933)

The author's father, Alasdair Nicolson, with his wife, Peggy (the author's stepmother), taken outside their home in Clachan, Raasay (late 1950s)

The author's aunt, Morag MacDonald, outside the house she built herself in Roag on Skye

The author and his wife shopping in Sauchiehall Street, Glasgow (1950)

The author, Catriona Nicolson and small boy. A picture postcard taken on Portree pier, Skye, in the mid 1960s. The author was unaware of its existence until he discovered it in a gift shop. The car he owned at the time (a grey Austin A40) is parked outside the shops at the extreme left of the picture.

The author's mother-in-law and father-in-law at their croft
in Borve on Skye (mid 1950s)

Retirement tribute to
the author

Brochel Castle, Raasay

The Church House, Torran, where the author was born

A commemorative bench donated by the Gaelic Society of London and erected as a memorial to the late author. The bench is situated on Raasay, overlooking no. 5 Oscaig, where he lived as a boy.

Raasay pier, reaching out towards Sconsor, Skye

Torran, Raasay, as it is today

'Brisco' had violet coloured eyes with long lashes and was a Don Juan among men. In the school playground he was a lanky lad who liked oatcakes. His lashes, like the rest of his body, grew up with him and his good looks were a genetic benefit bestowed on him through being related to my own ancestors. The men of Raasay were well known over the centuries for their manliness, an attribute reflected in a traditional song, the theme of which is the quality of the Raasay man's wedding tackle. The bestowal of this benefit carried the penalty of the fruits of inter-marriage over the years as the fair sex made sure that most males were bedded down on the island. Since those days, lassies from Skye and far away places like Lewis and Harris have claimed their share, and although Raasay males are nowadays in short supply, the quality is good and the blood mix is at least strong.

Blackie put us through our paces. The morning started with full class assembly singing the first two verses of Psalm 23 to the tune 'Crimond' and finished at four o'clock precisely with the singing of the first two verses of Psalm 121. Our teachers led the singing and were in fine voice. Blackie made full use of the blackboard and whatever other visual aids were available. He certainly held his class as he went through equations and theorems. Latin and Greek roots flowed freely and he introduced an element of passive gambling with stocks and shares. Outdoors, there were practical lessons in gardening. Vegetables had to be in neat straight lines and full use was made of spades, forks and hoes. Senior pupils were allocated little plots and lesser mortals were assigned to help them. Good quality vegetables were produced, not to mention parsley and other herbs. These sizeable parcels of ground were part of the schoolhouse garden, so with this exploitation of pupil performance, there was ample provision for a choice of vegetables for Sabbath lunch in the schoolhouse, no doubt also most useful during

Communion weekends when the headmistress provided hospitality to a never-ending stream of pious people, all of whom would have returned thanks.

Environmental study combined with local history provided further outdoor lessons. Blackie had an extensive knowledge of local history, going back for centuries – 'lost in the mists of antiquity' was how he used to refer to the history of Raasay. He sent us back into the sixth century with a visit to the Old Cemetery in Clachan where still can be seen the ancient ruins of a chapel. He held and stimulated our interest with a talk on the Brito-Celtic church of St Ninian, St Moluag's sojourn in Raasay and 'Chi-Rho Crosses'. One of the latter, stone incised and located nearby, was just another of his visual aids; but above all else, he had the ability to impart knowledge and hold the interest of his pupils. No doubt others like myself who were privileged to have been taught by him, regret not having made more of the opportunity to be better informed. (Some of his educational talent must have been inherited by his nephew, 'Calum the Road', Arnish, who himself was no mean exponent of Raasay's history and its people of a bygone age.) Nature study was also a serious part of our school roamings. In this sphere the Torran teachers were ahead. They were indeed knowledgeable. Foliage, flowers, frogs – all received coverage. Rita, our teacher, kept a colourful garden of marigolds, chrysanthemums, poppies and other annuals and perennials. Our small class was instructed to spend one Saturday searching for celandine:

> Tansies, Lilies, Kingcups, Daisies
> Let them live upon their praises;
> For the flower that shall be mine
> Is the little Celandine.

She had provided us with a pictorial description of celandine and buttercup. The petal formation was different and

116

other points were identified, relating to the stigma, style and ovary. We had other ideas about how Saturday should be spent. There was the call of the shore, the woodland and the streams, and there was tomorrow.

My sister and I were given permission to 'watch' the cows on the following morning – Sunday – a chore usually allocated to our brother Murdo or to our Uncle 'Trochan'. It was our Uncle's turn and he was only too ready to forego it. Our age-related cousins over the hill had no difficulty in swapping cow watching with their older brother. Suffice it to say that we produced more than one flower on Monday morning in class, assuring our teacher they were celandine. In our minds, we were convinced they were buttercups. We were given a fixed look but received no enlightenment. Our sacrilegious Sabbath day pickings had seen us through, by sheer accident or bluff! Teachers and lecturers nowadays are not required to have such a composite approach to pupil teaching as was in evidence in the 1930s and for some time thereafter. They may well be versed in general knowledge but, with respect, few would be able to impart knowledge over such a wide area of learning. The one and only teacher in many Highland schools, of which Torran was but one, had to be capable of dealing with school subjects covering an age-group of five to fourteen years. The range included: Bible study, spelling, transcription, dictation, composition, recitation, history, geography, grammar, English literature and language including roots, arithmetic including mental exercises, algebra, geometry, Gaelic, reading, writing, art, nature study in and out of doors, physical exercises, gardening, singing, handcrafts, cookery. Having mastered the alphabet, children were treated to word formation by use of 'sounds'.

In Torran school, the number of pupils at peak in the early 1930s was fifteen. Raasay school in mid-1939 had some fifty, but by October there was a massive influx of evacuees, mainly from Glasgow. They were of Glasgow–Island parentage. The teaching environment must have been strange for them but they adapted and integrated very well. They had to!

The teaching staff was increased to three and although, if only for logistic reasons, the teaching subjects were given an equitable 'spread', all the teachers were competent to deal with any of the subjects in the school curriculum. Blackie, to the dismay of some Glaswegians who had not yet become acquainted with Highland habits, carried on in full charge of the senior classes. His pointer soon kept everyone in line!

Not one to miss an opportunity, the end of the 1939 winter term debate, arranged by him as an innovation, was: 'Is country life better than town life?' Yours truly led for the affirmative, and after much lobbying, to the supposed annoyance of evacuee Anne Gillies, Pembroke Street, Glasgow, who spoke in support of town life, the country bumpkins won the debate with the withering comment, 'Why is Annie here?'

Prize giving followed the end-of-term debate. Books were presented as prizes. It was not the book itself that mattered but the fact that a prize had been awarded. A neatly designed certificate attached to the fly-sheet declared the name of the recipient, the school, class, date and the category of award – 1st, 2nd or 3rd Prize. If a cost-cutting exercise was needed, the certificate only would have been quite acceptable. The book simply gilded the lily and I believe that on occasions our teachers, dedicated to a fault, bought prize books out of their own pockets.

The end of term had arrived. I was now in my second year of Advanced Division II and was leaving school. Blackie did his utmost to convince me that I should stay on a little longer. We had an after-school chat. He did most of the talking. The only consolation in it for him would be the satisfaction of seeing one of his pupils do well. He could simply have gone home to his evening meal without further thought to my future. I appreciated much later what a kindly man he was and the degree of dedication that he evinced. Leaving school was a great feeling with no thought for lost opportunities and I did not take his advice. I thanked him profusely and my father wrote him a letter of appreciation which no doubt he qualified with suitable comment about the younger generation! I lived for the present and – like retirement from an active life – I realised in the years ahead that there was an unfulfilled yearning for what could not be attained.

The clock cannot go back: yesteryear will not return.

CHAPTER 4

CHURCH INFLUENCE

'The Public Means of Grace' were accepted as a way of life. Church services in Torran were held on most occasions by a lay preacher. During the 'Communion Weekend' in Raasay, Torran had a visitation from one of the officiating ministers. This was always on Thursday – 'Fast Day'. 'Feast Day' would have been a more appropriate description! There was much preparation for this event and it was an occasion when the Beatitudes were truly expounded. We had visions of being allowed no food for forty days and forty nights. This in practice was far from being the case. In later life when dealing with Asian seafarers, I found myself drawing a comparison between our Christian Fast Day with its unseemly display of food and their observance of Ramadan. East may not meet West but the various cultures on Earth have surely a common denominator.

The minister and many others ate lunch in our house, which was most convenient for them as our house was attached to the Mission House (church). The minister and other menfolk ate in the 'room' where everything was spotless for the occasion. They were served by some of the women 'guests' who, with Aunt Mary, ate in the kitchen – shades of Martha and Mary! The children received attention later. The lobby doors were kept open until grace was said by the minister. The arrangement was convenient and overcame the need for a woman to take on this function in the 'servant's quarters'. Man knew his place, woman knew her place – or at least so man thought! The teaching of St Paul to the Corinthians was seen to be practical. When the lobby doors closed, the kitchen scene soon changed, and unless a woman 'communicant' was present, the level of levity should not strictly have been for the ears of children.

There was always broth, thick with barley and vegetables and very tasty. Generous helpings of meat and potatoes boiled in their jackets followed, and for such a special occasion there was table jelly and tinned fruit for dessert. Tea, scones, oatcakes, jam, cheese and fresh butter rounded off the meal. The 'return of thanks' was said loudly and with much repetition by a male 'communicant'. These loud mutterings, were, like prayers, extempore, and gave the performer an opportunity – not to be missed – to show off. The womenfolk accepted that the Most High had been thanked also on their behalf and the volume of tobacco smoke curling into the lobby was the signal to clear the table. Aunt Mary made sure that we had our share of the mouth-watering goodies so, with a thought to our bellies, we went to church obediently and submitted ourselves to fearful exhortations with supporting remonstration and a degree of demonstration, depending on the style of the preacher.

Ministers such as John Colquhoun, James Macleod and John-Peter Macqueen, were on circuit and in great demand for communion seasons. Two of these, with sighs, signs and gesticulations, had the ability to hold the congregation spellbound. They had a turn of phrase which many might deem cruel and certainly instilled fear in the minds of some members of the congregation. 'Justice' was on a higher pedestal than 'Love' in the exposition of the Gospels. Ministers for some reason expounded three points during a sermon and dealt with them respectively at great length. It was never admitted nor denied that sermons were the subject of some homework by the good man in the pulpit, with probably the help of a concordance. Select portions of Scripture were (and still are) in vogue for special occasions and no funeral service would be complete without a portion of Psalm 90 being sung. It is of course a beautiful, free-flowing and sad psalm whether in prose or in metre. The emphasis is on man's frailty and the price that has to be paid for sin. The message from the minister was clear enough. We, as distinct from heathens, were privileged to be brought up in the land of the Gospel and more would be asked of us when the trumpet sounded – by inference, there are degrees of suffering in the bottomless pit. Millions the world over who from infinity were left off the Elected Roll, were disadvantaged and doomed from the start, so what was the point in praying? The privileged Elect would surely come to heel just as was the case with Saul of Tarsus.

An incident comes to mind when a youngster who was mentally retarded, died. I was distressed, as children tend to be in such situations and asked my uncle if the lad went to Heaven or to Hell. 'Oh well, nothing will be asked of him that he was not given' was the response. At least it indicated that I could not be given a definite answer, although, in my tender years, I did not appreciate the point. This kind of response was by no means in isolation and did suggest levels of pain and peace in eternity. What then is the lot of the millions who since the Creation, have passed on, without the benefit of the Gospel message? What about babes and little children who have not reached the age of understanding? Indeed what is the age of accountability?

Ours is not to reason why.

As youngsters, we were led to believe and expected to accept that God was speaking to the congregation through the preacher. God had gender and was male – that was one good reason why He could not communicate through a woman preacher. The point seemed logical enough in an age when Women's Lib had not yet been born. Nowadays

'Petticoat Penny' sees the church corporate as sexist and has even convinced the British Council of Churches that a study should be made of the 'sexist' language of the church. Well, I suppose that those who are tempted to follow this fashionable trend in feminism may feel that the headlines in Genesis, secured by their foremother Eve in her perfect state of disobedience and liking for fruit, entitles the female species to rib the establishment and end up with at least a neutered deity. The Roman Catholic church may have its own interpretation of the Second Commandment under Mosaic Law but the 'sexist' situation at least strikes a balance with intercession through Mother Mary. God in my own tiny little mind was white, but wait for it – colour coding will change all that. He also favoured the British Empire on which the sun in those days never set. We Britons were a privileged and favoured race – if not quite the chosen people.

Fast day came and went and we could be forgiven for thinking that with so much food about for the occasion, could we not have fast days more often! Everyone dressed for church. The ministers and lay preachers were in sombre black, complete with homburg for the journey. Visitors from Glasgow had bowler hats, usually manufactured by Dunns. 'Communicants', male and female, also wore severe dark clothes. Naturally, in our childhood ways we associated holiness on earth with the colour black, whilst those in Heaven and ghosts were always robed in white. Witches also wore black, as did Satan. As we grew older, we gave up colour comparisons and simply wondered where those in the beyond got their clothes from anyway. We knew that someone on earth was on to a good thing selling all these dark clothes, and, doubtless for material reasons, would always be on the lookout for more conversions.

The women were literally buttoned up and had their hair in severe buns. Betsy Cumming had to fasten her mother's corset complete with metal clips. Her job was twice as onerous when her holy auntie, a follower of fashions, was on holiday. She was well girthed. Aunt Annie went one better by not wearing any corsets as she grew older, and seemed to enjoy a state of emancipation until she had to go into mourning and fit back into the black dress kept especially for such an occasion by housewives. Catriona Graham got away with a hair coil to each side of her pretty face and enhanced her charm even further despite the sour looks from a *cailleach* (old woman) in Arnish. The severity of the hair bun suggested, to us children at any rate, degrees of holiness. Short hair and all facial adornment were infra dig and sinful. Earrings, provided they were plain gold ones, were acceptable, even although ear-piercing constituted body abuse!

In the strict Presbyterian churches, the congregation remains seated during the singing. Only the precentor stands and psalms only, in metre, are sung. Psalms are the 'inspired Word of God'; that is why they and not para-phrases or hymns are used. The Book of Psalms is of course in prose but that is a minor point. During prayers, of which there are usually two, the first very long and the latter very short, the congregation stands – other than some older persons for whom it is permissible and the fashion to sit down after some ten minutes 'on their feet'. In private worship, which was conducted twice daily in my childhood, the family kneels during devotions. It is confusing, to say the least, as to why there is this variance in procedure and on what authority it is based. Times and customs do not change greatly and one is left wondering what really motivates many people to attend church. Is it because it is the done thing? Dresses and hats are talking points with the women and the men are not above passing comment either. Old Janet falls asleep and there is a rustle and a clatter as the proverbial 'imperial' sweet, so popular with churchgoers, drops through limp and tired fingers. Where is the 'Fisherman's Friend'?

During the first half of the twentieth century some Highland ministers received hero worship. They were idolised, usually by women, and often by older women suffering from either frustration or a 'crush on the minister'. A framed photograph of the minister in his sartorial finery and with a pious expression, if that can be defined, was often to be seen on the mantelpiece of 'the room' in many homes. In crofthouses the room had the best furniture, and although it was fitted with one and sometimes two double beds, it was used for special guests at mealtimes.

This hero worship of clerics bordered on the profane and a breach of the second commandment. There were even occasions when offspring were named after the minister! Names such as Donald Macfarlane and Neil Cameron – both powerful preachers – were quite common, and one is left wondering what the man of the house thought. No doubt he had sin in his heart and counted the months, if he was a sailor!

Preachers were not above entering the political arena and dealing with current affairs. Indeed, some seemed to show off their knowledge of national events, but then they read the national newspapers (except the Sunday ones), didn't they? Later on, it became fashionable not to read the Monday papers because they were printed on the Sabbath. This terrible discovery had not been made in my own schooldays and our Sabbath-observing school teacher blithely bought by subscription and read Monday's *Bulletin*, which always arrived on Wednesday. Preachers were not, however, so ready to introduce past Highland history into their sermons, except to denigrate Graham of Claverhouse and others of his ilk. It has often seemed to me, on reflection, that both at home and in school, we were left to assume that the events of the '45 ended with Culloden. We knew about the Pretender's romantic roamings in Skye and that he had been in hiding in Raasay, but for some inexplicable reason the subsequent rape of Raasay and Rona by Cumberland's troops was glossed over. It had all taken place within two hundred years – not a long time in terms of history, and there was still plenty of evidence of pillaged croft houses – or was the evidence that of the infamous evictions which followed in even more recent times? Could it be that because the natives of these islands held other beliefs in those days, their terrible sufferings were forgotten too readily by successive generations?

The Commandments taught us to obey and respect authority. In our young minds we placed preachers on a pedestal. Those who preached the Word gave scant comfort to crofters, conveniently relating obedience to authority, to suit the occasion. One could be forgiven for wondering how the activities of Moses and many of the biblical prophets and holy men of the New Testament could be reconciled to the theology as expounded by these preachers. Times have not changed greatly and in these latter years of the twentieth century we can find preachers who talk parrot fashion about Christian duty and national powers that are ordained from on high when emotive subjects such as war bases come in for discussion. It may have been of course that this obscene part of Highland history was blanked off by our parents because of their own feelings of revulsion. There is some reason to believe that the owners of estates where outrages had been committed went to some lengths and expense acquiring and destroying any literature that was descriptive of the Clearances.

Raasay suffered virtually a reign of terror after Culloden and during the Clearances. It should not be forgotten that crofters in Raasay and many parts of the Highlands and islands owe their fairly comfortable existence nowadays to the stand made by their predecessors in support of crofting

126

rights. Families perished of starvation, were removed from the shack-dwellings they erected for themselves, dispossessed of any land and ordered to leave their crofting communities without prior notice before the passing of the Crofters' Act in 1886. In order to achieve what can be regarded as a matter of basic human rights there had to be a 'Battle of the Braes', the 'Glendale Martyrs' and many other incidents of agitation, including the imprisonment of crofters. Many of the Highland Land Leaguers were devout Christians who kept faith with their consciences, and toiled and suffered much for the way of life that some of their descendants now take for granted.

In Raasay alone no fewer than twelve crofting townships were cleared of crofters, no horse other than that of the landlord was allowed on the island and no marriage could take place without the landlord's express permission. One house was razed to the ground because the occupants had disobeyed this latter evil edict. These are frightening facts about what occurred in a supposedly civilised nation and were a great intrusion on the dignity of the human race. Explicit details may be read in various publications including *The Scottish Highlander* of 1893.

Through all these traumatic experiences most church leaders went sing-a-long. Ecclesiastics preached about obedience to authority (supposedly) divinely appointed. The materialism of ministers of religion did not escape the pens of historians. Church land (glebes), already extensive, were enlarged further following the wholesale eviction of crofters:

> Ill fares the land, to hastening ills a prey,
> Where wealth accumulates and men decay.

Dire warnings were proclaimed systematically from the pulpit, to such as might at any time feel disposed to criticise 'those whom God has chosen'. This in-built protectionism of the 'Elect' has back-fired over the years, and even in narrow church circles the level of brotherly and sisterly love has been strained to breaking point, ending in protest, schism and secession. A very serious view indeed is taken of a fellow minister's 'Protest', by the synod of strict Presbyterians. The attitude displayed seems, to the layman at any rate, to fall short in the area of brotherly love.

Some church-goers in the Highlands and islands have, over the years, taken their chance, and despite fear of 'the wrath to come', have openly criticised 'the man of God'. Torran was no exception. Away back in 1932, the men from Fladda set about repairing the mission-house in Torran, at a time when spring was in the air. Donald Graham, who has already received mention in 'The Opening Years' (Chapter 1), and others, felt that the work, which was extensive, should be held over until later, when the church could be a community effort. These differences were not reconciled amicably, and sadly, ended up in the Courthouse, Portree.

'God will defend me,' said one young fellow from Fladda, to the Sheriff.
'My good fellow,' responded the Sheriff, 'I would advise you to take on someone more local.'

The lay preacher from Fladda was accused of using the pulpit to get at the objectors. As a result, the congregation was split and there was acrimony. The customary invitation to lunch between church services, for those living in far away places such as Fladda, was no longer forthcoming from those living in Torran and Arnish, most of whom did not attend church when the Fladda lay preacher conducted the service. We were the exception and our house was like a guest house on the Sabbath day, often with some twenty persons for lunch. My father took a neutral stance and kept an open door for all comers. There were those, to their discredit, who tried to have our family removed from the mission dwelling house, for no other reason than that my father provided hospitality to the Fladda people. Aunt Mary was often very tired even although the guests helped with the food.

We were taught to 'keep the Sabbath day holy and do no work'. I could not comprehend how this philosophy related to what went on. The break between church services became a social event with the exchange of news and idle chatter. How could it be otherwise? I suspect that much the same still happens on the Sabbath at Communion 'seasons' when there is a houseful of guests, many of whom have not met for months previously. 'So what!' you may say. It has to be seen in context. Everyone in North Raasay belonged to a strict Presbyterian sect where Sabbatarianism ruled. It was the prime Commandment, or so it seemed to me. After all, no-one committed murder, there was no adultery, at least openly, though cousin John and I once stumbled on a courting couple who aroused our curiosity by their activities in a gravel pit near the 'Wooden Gate' (*Geata na Coille*). Nearly everyone coveted from Price Lists, a *cailleach* or two indulged in *tapags* (expletives) and terminological inexactitudes, and those who may unwittingly have taken a sheep or two or three, were shortsighted, albeit long in the arm, and could not distinguish between their own property and that of others. The latter of course did not belong to North Raasay, and more than likely came from Skye anyway, where from time to time sheep rustling was known to take place!

The Fladda lay preacher took to his bed and a mason missionary replaced him, much to the satisfaction of the Arnish community and some others. He lived in South Raasay, and because of his work as a builder he had perforce to make the two-way journey on the Sabbath day. This involved the use of the shoemaker's car. There were those who asked if the actual hire was paid for on the Sabbath. Anyway, the need for a preacher dominated the scene and the shoemaker, being a sensible and practical person, did not deny that he made no money out of these excursions. After all, he stocked petrol and supplied it to himself. He never took Communion! The missionary naturally had free lunch in our house. He also had a cup of tea on arrival and another to sustain him on his three-mile walk back to Brochel Castle after the service, blow high or low. He was regarded as a powerful preacher, a nice man who suffered the little children. We always enjoyed his handful of clove-filled peppermints. Whatever has happened to that confection?

Despite the unfortunate disharmony among the congregation in such a small community, where most people were related, church pressures were probably less pronounced in Torran in my formative years than in other island townships. There were no Sunday school sessions in Torran in my time and on many Sundays over a decade no church services were held. While we were expected to pass the time of day reading 'good books', we soon tired of *The Pilgrim's Progress*, and the monthly church magazine's main interest for us lay in the section which listed those who had donated to numerous funds. The Sustentation Fund, Church Repair Funds, Manse Building Funds and the Foreign Missions' Fund are some that come to mind. The National Bible Society was also listed, but in later years, for some doctrinaire reason, financial support was switched to the Trinitarian Bible Society. The donations lists were sprinkled with quotes from Scripture, used as noms de plume, and we were fascinated and for some time puzzled by the obviously very rich person called Anon, who appeared in every list – sometimes with repetitive regularity in the same list! It was years later before the church got round to producing a Young People's Magazine which, with its competitions, at least had some appeal, even if it lacked pictorial presentation. Journalistic flair was not much in evidence and a good deal of the prose was as dry as the east wind.

Spurgeon's Sermons were for older people, so our youthful

energy found outlets elsewhere. Every household held family worship after breakfast and last thing at night. Some called it private worship – which it was not. The act of worship last thing at night was to ensure that every member of the family was at home at a reasonable hour and took to bed after the last knee was lifted. It did not always work out that way in parts of Lewis. It was the signal for the young men to disappear by way of the unlatched door or closet window and make for the hills and the *bothan* (drinking den – unlicensed and illegal). It was an all-night affair. In colder weather, it was a different sport, and they gained entry into the bedrooms of local lassies, and in next to no time took part in the traditional pastime known as 'bundling'. It was all done by passive parental consent, and very soon afterwards sheep and hens were earmarked for nuptials.

One young island sailor took unto himself a wife from Liverpool. At the marriage service, with the bride in white and the groom in blue, kneeling side by side in front of the altar, there for all to see was number 14 chalked on the soles of both pairs of shoes.

Those who had failed to appreciate the significance of what they had seen, knew nothing of the ways of a hotel bootboy! 'What else could you expect of a lass from Liverpool?' said one old *cailleach* at a ceilidh. 'I used to hear my late husband talk about the ladies from Lime Street, as he used to put it.' 'Put what?' said another. 'Well, she should have got married in a Presbyterian church'. Significantly, had the young couple done so, their secret would have been safe, as vows and prayers are presented with both feet solidly on terra firma. Perhaps the old woman was not such a bigot after all!

My father, as head of the household, said grace before and after meals. If he was not at home, then the oldest male, if of mature age, took over; otherwise, it was the turn of a woman. These were unwritten rules and were observed with some rigidity. Cups of tea – morning and afternoon, and at ceilidhs, also the odd dram – all qualified for grace. A male visitor, when partaking of food, liquid or otherwise, was usually invited to say grace on behalf of everyone present and expected to accept the privilege, other than in instances when the head of the household was a church 'member' or a 'good man'. The visitor was expected to be heard by mortals as well as by God.

I recall the occasion when a retired minister of great grace and charm used to visit my father and stepmother in Clachan, Raasay. She, bless her, had the fried fish ready for plating immediately after grace was said. The honoured guest went into geographical detail in his one-sided discourse with the Almighty, ending up with a vivid description of the beautiful bens of Skye, before setting off at some pace to deal with the state of the nation. 'Amazing Grace' indeed! When at last we tucked into the fried haddock, it was no longer juicy. The minister said that it was very good and I am sure that he said so sincerely. I was not too enchanted, much as I liked the old fellow who was a regular and welcome visitor and a bit lonely. He had great charisma and was a scholar in the truest sense of the word. We arrived at the ultimate when, with the food on the table, we had a second dissertation. Thereafter, my father, wicked man, said grace on such occasions but he retained the custom of inviting a male guest to 'return thanks'.

'Thanks' were always returned after meals. Grace and thanks complemented each other like bacon and eggs. It was a ritualistic and parrot-like performance. If the weather was good and croft work was calling, family worship was remarkably short! Prayers and grace were sometimes a bit theatrical, to impress visitors, rather than the Most High. On challenging my father, whose contributions I could not hear, and Uncle Donald who prattled on at an impossibly fast and unintelligible pace, I was reminded, with a twinkle in their eyes, that their implorings were to Him who sits in the Heavens high, who knew what was in their hearts, and that their faith needed to be no more than a grain of mustard seed. Still, they had both been sailors.

The full church service comprised the reading of three psalms, followed in each instance by the precenting and singing of four, three and two verses respectively. A long prayer followed the singing of the first psalm, then a portion of scripture was read, followed by the reading and singing of the next psalm. At this stage of the proceedings there was much rustling of pokes of peppermints, followed by a surreptitious handout along the whole pew. Singing sitting had its advantages and the singing did at least appear to reduce the rustle to a respectable level. The preacher on his pedestal read again part of the portion of scripture that he had read previously, and after due modulation of voice, if he was a minister, he took off with his 'three points of fellowship'. If he was a mere lay preacher it was considered presumptuous of him to define points in scripture for preaching and in most cases the congregation were then subjected to a lengthy intonation which lacked coherence. In some instances, when least expected by the congregation, the sermon came to an abrupt end, and without further ado everyone was on their feet for the second prayer, which was quite short, unless it happened to be a 'guest prayerer' on such occasions as fast days and the Glasgow Fair, when this part of the service was something of a show-off.

Despite being moved by the spirit, time as well as motion were taken into account by the preacher and reference was actually made to a pocket-watch which the preacher prior to entering the church had removed from his waistcoat pocket and, on making himself comfortable in the pulpit, had placed on a triangular wooden ledge in line with the lectern and out of sight of all others but himself. His next act was to gaze or glare – depending on interpretation – usually over the top of his spectacles, handed down from generation to generation, at the sea of faces in the pews below.

There were those among us who with monotonous regularity found it convenient to have upset stomachs on Saturday and in consequence needed to take medicine later in the day. The Sabbath morning service just had to be missed – and the cows kept getting into the corn! However, all was well for the evening service which for some reason was shorter than the one in the morning, especially on wet wintry nights, and according to the state of the tide, if the preacher came from Fladda. Many who attended church came some distance, and although spiritual welfare was anticipated, the time was not yet and the creature comforts afforded through a shorter evening service were God's will, and the consideration – through the preacher – was appreciated and acknowledged on bended knees before bedtime.

No church service would be complete without a collection. Fast on the heels of the last prayer, the collection box was on its way. It was attached to a thin pole, longer than a broom handle, presumably to make contact with the far end of each pew. The collector used a prodding movement which he had developed and perfected through herding the cattle over many years and there was no escape! The procedure at least had a personal touch and the value of the offering could be related, if one wished, to the value attributed to the sermon – not like the latter-day practice of being relieved of a donation at the church entrance. If, perchance, the preacher had overrun his time – a regular occurrence – and probably feeling that the congregation had by now been divested of all their metallic substance, he only read the first two lines of the first of two verses that he had selected for the last psalm of the service. The precentor took over and gave them a quick dispatch. In the absence of a minister, a lay preacher did not give the benediction but concluded with the words 'we shall not be waiting any longer at this time' ('cha bhi sinn a' fuireach nas fhaide aig an am so'). It is not clear why a minister only should pronounce the benediction but it is thought to be a throw-back to Judaistic times when synagogue ritual decreed that the high priest and the high priest only, would pronounce a blessing.

Once outside, there were many 'hallos' and invitations to lunch, in subdued and decorous tones. These impromptu meetings at the church door were accepted as a way of life in Torran, but not so in the South Raasay church. The practice, at least in my boyhood days, was frowned upon by 'holy' people who could be seen taking off at great speed in case they should be laid open to temptation on the Sabbath. A near-run was bad enough as it was an unwritten commandment that no-one must run on the Sabbath day. In some cases, theological belief on this scale in no small way preserved the contents of the larder.

The old and not so old from Fladda had a stock answer to the enquiry about their health – 'there is no cause to complain' ('chan eil còir a bhith gearain'). This response implied that whilst the person might not be too well – and Fladda did seem to have an unusual number of hypochondriacs, although stomach upsets were real enough – others were worse off, and the affliction of indifferent health was after all the just desserts of a human race who were branded with original and actual sin. It was a subconscious acceptance of penance, and suffering whether in body or mind was a sinner's privilege and indicative of some atonement. Coming into the world with the burden of original sin must place an undue strain on the stork! It does seem an unjust imposition as we are on earth without any say in the matter. Original sin continues to be one of the focal points in sermons, by inference making procreation unclean – a mere pleasure of the flesh.

Other phrases in common use to this day are 'God Willing' (DV) and 'if spared'. Coming from 'good-living' people it seems to be a contradiction. Spared from what? As a place in the hereafter is assured, death should have no sting. Letters accepting invitations and holiday postcards are sprinkled with DVs and have nothing in common with the Motor Vehicle Licensing Centre in Swansea. These careful people appear to regard life not so much as a gift but as a loan, which may be called in without notice, even although they believe that to be free from the fear of the grim reaper is a gift of the spirit.

At the age of seventy, you were a marked person. Three score and ten was your allotted span – with a bit of luck you might chalk up four score. Beyond that – oh well, 'he – or she – had been given a big world' ('Fhuair e saoghal mór'), was a favourite expression. Some said it in a way that suggested the poor soul did not deserve such munificence.

Cremation was the ultimate insult to the body. It was seen as a procedure instituted by atheists to circumvent the unification of the body and soul at the resurrection. It was considered to have no backing in scripture, even if, according to the Book of 1st Samuel, it was a fate that befell Saul and his sons. Preacher after preacher emphasised that we were dust and that to dust we would return and so remain until the trumpet sounded and we would all rise at the Day of Judgement. Ah well – the worms made the most of it anyway.

Church Services in Torran were in Gaelic, other than during the Glasgow Fair holiday, when the lay preacher said a few words in English 'for the benefit of the visitors'. It was an addition to the full service – a translation of the sermon, delivered with a confusion of pronouns and mixed metaphors. It is doubtful if the consideration extended by the preacher was appreciated either by the Glaswegians or the locals. It certainly was not appreciated by Aunt Mary who, seeing to lunch, used to stand out of sight by the adjacent church window waiting for the start of the second and shorter prayer of the service. It was her signal for boiling the potatoes, in a massive cast-iron pot, so that they were just cooked by the time the family and guests got into the house. There was quite a knack in draining such a large pot of potatoes, but it was done well, and a clean teacloth placed under the lid ensured that the potatoes were dry-steamed and produced wide floury smiles on the large willow-patterned ashet which conveyed them to the table. The broth only needed reheating and the meat was served cold as these had been cooked the night before with a thought to 'works of necessity and mercy'. No-one would have dreamed of eating cold potatoes in any form, and cooking them just before eating was conveniently accepted as a work of mercy if not one of necessity!

During the Glasgow Fair holiday, a Gaelic-speaking elder from Glasgow was invited to take over as precentor. After feigning some surprise, he took over, complete with a tuning fork which he always produced from the top pocket of the waistcoat of a double-breasted suit which became more highly glossed as the years went by. Some of the tunes were thought to be rather trendy by the older folk who took to squeaking at the high notes. We youngsters enjoyed their embarrassment as much as the innovation. The elder, with long service in the Clyde Trust, was a kindly man but a most inquisitive one. Even if his thoughts were on higher things he had no qualms about delving into other people's pay-rates and such matters as the number of sheep on the hill. His nosiness came in for some comment, but he was now a pillar of society although, said some, he could have qualified for a 'column' in the *News of the World*, had that paper existed in his younger days!

Panac, whose husband was the precentor in residence, complained, so some said, with green in her eyes, that music was being used in God's house and that her own Calum who put his trust in God and not in the Clyde, had no need of a

137

chorus fork or whatever fancy name was used by these Glasgow Highlanders for the two-pronged musical instrument with a knob on the end of it. Her tirade hit a flat note. The Clyde Trust tenor was a popular person and his friends and relatives were many. Panac's interpretation of music was off-key, but perhaps a fork, by whatever name, savoured too much of Lowland ways for her liking. Gossip had it that she harnessed the striking mechanism of the kitchen pendulum-clock on Saturday night, so that its chimes did not disturb the peace of the Sabbath.

The use of a microphone by a preacher in church is even to this day viewed with reservations by some church-goers. Others, a shade hard of hearing, concede grudgingly that the gospel message comes across loudly, if not always too clearly. The process is probably one of evolution – in itself a dirty word with strict Presbyterians. Whatever the differing points of view that may be held about the projection of the human voice by mechanical means, strict Presbyterians are in accord on the subject of music in church. The singing of alleluia is by vocal chord, and musical accompaniment is on no account permitted.

The pews in Torran were numbered. Ours was number seven, about halfway up the aisle. Donald Graham and his family sat immediately in front of us. Whenever the sermon lacked fire and brimstone or went on for too long, there was always the distraction of the seabirds and the fish jumping in Loch Arnish, all clearly visible from both these pews. The windows were plain glass. Panac, the old lady from Brae, who was married to the regular precentor and was privileged to have a side pew, watched everyone's twitch and suggested quite seriously that the windows should be boarded up so that Donald Graham in particular was not led into temptation – after all, he owned a fishing boat! Floral arrangements, even for weddings, are never to be seen inside a strict Scottish Presbyterian church and Torran was no exception. Wreaths, although nowadays not openly discouraged, are not viewed with great favour. Like Christmas trees they are seen at worst as popish symbols and at best as fripperies which could well be in breach of the Second Commandment!

Old Ruaridh and his wife Kate, on annual holiday from Glasgow, sat in the pew in front of Donald Graham. Ruaridh, who partook of the Lord's Supper, when invited to engage in prayer, tended to sniffle outrageously and was distinctly long-winded. His contribution was often shortened by his better half who was not slow in administering a strong kick to his shin. This was common knowledge, and we awaited the moment of impact, which could be heard distinctly, with some amusement. There is no evidence that she belonged to Women's Lib. The Macleods from Fladda sat immediately behind us and their contribution to the service was their ability to sing. Had the younger set been trained, they could well have won acclaim at the National Mods. It was not always psalms that were sung over the hills and far away.

Saturday was a day of great preparation for the Sabbath. Table knives, which in the early thirties were mild steel, had to be polished. There was a special board and fine sand or ash for this purpose. The freshwater cask was full to the brim, as were two, and sometimes more, enamel or tin pails. No one talked of buckets. Boots and shoes were polished until they gleamed. Boxes of peat and sticks, kept under the bench and in a corner between it and the end wall, were filled to overflowing. We children provided most of the labour and there was no pocket money! The ash was sometimes removed from the hearth in the late evening, as this was not a work of necessity for the morrow. If the hens were in a mood they were placed under a creel for the whole weekend, just in case the cockerel became too frisky. By the same token, it was not considered sinful to have a cow serviced on the Sabbath – providing it was not done during church hours of service; there must have been some kind of dispensation even if it was not a papal bull! It was permissible to milk the cattle but not to collect the eggs. These man-made rules were broken furtively. Little escaped our eyes and ears. Nets and lobster pots were landed on Saturday, and as a last duty grown-up males shaved before bedtime. So ended the sixth day.

Some who professed to be Christians had a narrow and indeed bigoted approach to life. If a disaster befell a 'member' of the church, it was 'God's will'. If it befell someone who liked a dram or had some other apparent shortcoming, it was 'punishment from on High'. A 'member' of the church incidentally was not simply a regular church-goer or someone who donated to the sustentation or other of the many church funds. It was not that simple. Although it was predestined and part of the Doctrine of Election, a 'member' had to be 'saved' and seen to be saved. 'By their deeds ye shall know them' was a favourite expression. The person always wore dark clothes, sighed deeply in the initial stage of conversion and partook of communion wine. It did not escape our notice as we grew older that some families appeared to have been favoured and had many 'members'. Life could not have been comfortable for the odd one out! Could it have been a kind of status symbol when other families carried on as unforgiven sinners? There was considerable excitement at communion seasons when new adherents partook of communion and their worthiness was analysed, often critically, over some supper tables. Either way, there was often a strong presumption peppered with prejudice. Even the Ten Commandments had due allocation. The first four were for God and the remainder set behavioural standards on earth.

The Sabbath day was undoubtedly the God-spot of the week, and the physical involvements leading up to its observance as a day of rest suggested that 'man was made for the Sabbath'! The attitude of these 'holy' people reminded me in later life of the old rhyme:

> We are God's chosen few;
> Let all the rest be damned.
> There is no room in Heaven for you,
> We cannot have it crammed.

One old enthusiast crossed out the word 'Sunday' from her many calendars and substituted the word 'Sabbath'. How the dilemma of the first day of the week being the seventh day was reconciled, is not on record. She certainly knew nothing about the Council of Laodicea. We assumed in our own simple way that in the Beyond, which we accepted to be somewhere above the clouds, there was a balancing of the 'big book' – which, we were often told, contained all our names and deeds – by means of some census system. It would all be in Gaelic naturally. Our approach to life was understandably parochial in our closed environment. There was also a gullible approach by our elders to real life and it was related to scripture beyond a reasonable level of imagination. A young prankster from Arnish placed potatoes by the pailful in the ground below some shoots, whilst his old Uncle Calum was having lunch and his usual nap. On return to his labours after due digging with his Highland hoe (*croman*), he came across what seemed an unending crop. He there and then dropped to his knees, looked skyward and chanted a biblical quotation 'Is t'obair-s' a Dhé tha iongantach' (Thy works Oh Lord are wonderful) believing completely that he had been specially favoured! What a superiority complex, even if they were the best of 'Kerr's Pinks'!

Those responsible for Christian teaching through the church took every opportunity to analyse the faults in other factions who also professed presbyterianism. Episcopalians and Roman Catholics were lost anyway and had no chance of salvation unless they repented and became strict presbyterians. The pope came in for special attention and was often referred to as 'that man of sin'. Could he possibly have been excluded when man was created in God's own image? The Free Church of Scotland, from which a substantial portion of the congregation had seceded in 1893 because of some disagreement over Darwin and his monkey business, was also in the firing line. There was and still is a small Free Church congregation in the South end of Raasay. At the time of these church ructions their preacher, it was said, proclaimed in Gaelic, 'These seceders think that no one will go to Heaven but themselves. Ha ha – wouldn't I laugh if no-one went there'! Hot stuff! Heard by a Gaelic speaker, this quotation is most expressive. It certainly seemed to cast doubt on, if not even to disprove, the theory of some comfort in the hereafter.

During my time at sea I heard even more about the hereafter from a Highland sailor:

There was this youngish old maid from Tigh-na-Bruaich (the house on the brae) who, after the mid-week prayer meeting, complimented the minister on his sermon, but added that he referred a great deal to the hereafter and she would appreciate an exposition.

'Well, well, my good woman, you come with me.'

Off they went over the hills and the heather until she was tired out.

'Where are we going, Reverend Mr Macleod? – and you have not explained to me about the "hereafter".'

'Now sit you down in this hollow, Miss Macallinish and I shall explain all; "if you're here after what I'm here after, we're both here after the same – but if you're not here after what I'm here after, then you'll be here, after I'm hame".'

She saw the stars in a new dimension and accepted the minister's penetrating exposition.

The place of worship in South Raasay where we made our devotions after moving to Oscaig, is a real church as distinct from a meeting-house such as we had in Torran. It is said to be built true east to west which in itself has some symbolic significance. It is not particularly picturesque in its prominent position on high ground, overlooking the 'school park' and the Sconser Quarry. The church, built in 1929, has a vestry and a front porch. In Torran, the door of the place of worship was never locked – and to my knowledge there was no abuse. Here, the door is always locked except when there is a service being held or some maintenance work is in hand. This practice is not peculiar to Raasay but may be observed in many rural areas. There is no open door, unlike, paradoxically, some city churches where there is no such impediment to worshippers, whatever their denomination, carrying out their devotions for many hours of the day.

The collection plate for an offering, resting on a small table by the porchway entrance, confronts one inanimately on the way in. There are no niceties such as passing the plate for an offering and a subsequent blessing by the preacher. The pews are more accommodating than was the case in Torran and cushioned seats seem no longer to be frowned upon! There are no footrests and of course no prayer mats. Shortly after our move to Oscaig, the church could claim a full house, due to the influx of evacuees. One of my earliest recollections was seeing among the congregation, a retired well-constructed male and his diminutive Welsh wife who could barely be seen by his side as they climbed the road over the steep hill leading to the church in my opposite direction. Why she was such a regular church attender was a mystery, as she could not understand Gaelic and few church services were then in English. Both had sartorial style. Murdo, the husband, was a massive man who had retired to Raasay from the Glasgow police, where in his service days he had gained considerable notoriety as a prankster. As a young man in Rona he did not always get his way, and in retaliation more than one unwilling maiden found a live conger eel wriggling among her bedclothes. These days were long gone and now, dressed in tweeds, highly polished shoes and spats, he could not be missed in a crowd. This couple may not have been a natural match but they were in accord when it came to style. Plus-fours were fashionable but those they did not suit looked an odd sight in church – far more so than the jeans worn by the youth of today.

In later years one of my own sisters-in-law did not respond to the favours of a young, well established Raasay man, simply because she took an instant dislike to his plus-fours. Her sister, of a more practical disposition, took her chance and married Torquil, one of my many cousins. His plus-fours, which he had often worn to church, were last seen, within weeks of the wedding, in a field of turnips adorning a scarecrow.

The sectarianism of self-righteousness in the church's teaching was oppressive and indefensible. A visiting minister, on one occasion when I attended church, declared from the pulpit that it was a mortal sin for anyone in the congregation to marry a person not of the same denomination. Preaching through fear has far too often led to deep depression, known in Highland circles as the 'curam' (care). Like alcoholism, it is an ailment which in extreme cases requires specialist treatment in hospital. Craig Dunain was the best known of these hospitals in the Highlands and islands of Scotland, where there has been ample evidence over many years of the effects of a narrow upbringing. Youngsters, after finding city jobs, have in record time abandoned their former forced way of life, replacing it with less than acceptable standards in some instances. The children of my generation, who grew up with me in Torran, seem on the whole to have been more fortunate, due to the understanding of our elders (even if they were not always as

144

forthcoming as they should have been), and in no small measure to teacher care. In our formative years we read with relish Bible stories about wars and the general afflictions of mankind, all of which seemed to be glorified through Christian teaching. There was some emphasis on vengeance and it was unchristian and unthinkable that capital punishment, for example, could ever be abolished! It was doom and gloom from womb to tomb – and worse for many of us in the beyond if we were not on the register of the 'Elect'.

Some others with their passage booked for Shangri La seemed anything but at peace with themselves. Did they harbour secret doubts? Their way of life centred on the Sabbath. Indeed, the tranquillity that the Sabbath day brought in a place like Torran was an experience that I in my own childhood did not appreciate. Monday meant school but it could not come quickly enough. I am convinced that many of the older folk sinned in thought on Sunday evenings by willing the day away. Why else did they go to bed earlier than on the other nights of the week?

As we passed through early adolescence, with a strictly limited access to books of knowledge, we read the Bible for the wrong reasons. We shared the sentiments of Oscar Wilde when he wrote, 'As the Bible begins with a man and woman in a garden it naturally ends with Revelations'. Erotic excitement was to be found in parts of Deuteronomy, Isaiah and other portions of scripture such as those that record the amorous activities of David and Solomon. It is nothing of which to be proud but it is honest and 'confession is good for the soul'. Youth will have its fling and keeping the seamier side of life under wrappers, as if it did not exist, however good the intentions of home and church, is a short-term and futile exercise.

Some church-goers could truly be classified as pulpit poodles, and their patronising patter struck a sour note over the years. Church-goers who were true believers lived for the church – it was an important part of their lives which provided their spiritual life-blood, and they derived succour and support from the reading, singing, preaching and teaching of the Word. They believed implicitly in the power of prayer and the message of the gospel as they interpreted it through the preacher. Indeed, they followed a way of life which had no discernible blemish. They were kindly, courteous and sincere. They had time for us young people who were around them, and by deeds and words showed concern for our material and spiritual welfare. It could be said that the motto of each one of them was 'above all else to thine own self be true'.

I was privileged to have enjoyed their company during the formative years of my life and I cherish their memory – people like Kate, Janet, Neil and Norman – poor and penniless as they so often were, but richly endowed with spiritual blessings which over the years seem to have eluded me.

The church, our upbringing and in the much wider sense, an appreciation of the teachings of the Bible, which has something for everyone, have influenced our lives, but the direction of influence is not uniform. We became men and women and went our different ways. Some of the children who grew up with me have followed in their parents' footsteps and appear to lead full and happy lives, in some cases even in indolence. It was a natural reaction even if perhaps a passive decision, for had we not often been commanded to 'Remember thy creator in the days of thy Youth'. Doing so was seen as carrying on in the sectarian style of our childhood. Others, like myself, think that we have 'broadened' our thinking, but conversely our approach may be due to earlier church influence also. Taking 'one day at a time' is fine in the peace of a croft haven; but life is real, life is earnest, and forward planning on a much bigger timescale without such considerations as Deo Volente, are business processes – perhaps another penalty of our sins. The world, perhaps unfortunately, is a bigger place than a few crofts scattered among Highland hills where, if only because of the closeness to nature, one could be excused for assuming that there are near exclusive privileges, with Valhalla in mind, conferred by the Almighty – a chosen people, circumscribed through insularity. What presumption, saith the Jews!

As my own vision broadened, the church, which I was brought up to believe to be the body of Christ, seemed to dwell on and preach about individual morality, whilst the many factions in it across the world of Christendom appeared to lack corporate morality. There was a lack of love and trust just as was the case with nations. Despite much preaching of the Word, and in the knowledge that we were destined to die, landing – we were told – in one of two places, we were a complacent lot. Outpourings in prayer both in church and in the home suggested to me that we were very demanding of God to the point of presumption and selfishness. Church sermons in my own formative years struck me as over-emphasising justice and vengeance in the context of a common denominator. What about taking up a stance of non-violence – turning the other cheek? This also was part of the scriptures. Surely, it was not merely an ideal. Having fallen from favour, unbeknown to ourselves, was rather unfortunate, but the church, fortunately for those elected, also preached about redemption. Could we perchance contribute to it by our own human endeavour? Saved sinners could afford to be smug and patronising. They apparently knew something even denied to those of us in a world of darkness visible – a 'Catch 22' situation.

Although Lord Hailsham went even further in his letter to *The Times* in November 1988, belief in the Bible as the inspired word of God is not necessarily reconciled to such church laws as are man-made, even if these are based on

'The Westminster Confession of Faith'. The use of psalms and not hymns in worship may be a fair analogy.

In his book, *Parachute Padre – Behind the German Lines with the SAS, France 1944*, the Revd J. Fraser McLuskey, MC, gives a vivid exposition on the subject of worship, sharing as he did with other brave men, in a common and raw environment, the various expeditions, the vigils, the chances, the fears and the same hopes.

In the final analysis, our way of life in public and in private is a matter of conscience, admittedly governed by acceptable standards and within the law of the land to which we owe allegiance. We are no better and no worse than millions of people the world over who practise different creeds and hold different cultures. Dissension over matters relating to public worship such as the interpretation of the sacraments, whether to stand or sit when singing the praises of the Lord, the use of hymns as well as psalms, whether to pray in a standing, sitting or kneeling position, the use of music and baptism by immersion at an adult age, or merely by the sprinkling of water over the heads of infants, are surely but trivial when it comes to consider 'man's chief end'. It is indeed a sad reflection on Christianity and other religions the world over, that wars and much cruelty, physical and mental, have to be laid at the door of dogma.

In school, we played games of make-believe, some of us acting the part of 'holy' people and spicing our dialogue with phrases which were slanderous and probably blasphemous as well. We could not, even at that tender age, be unaware of church dissension, and our imagination led us to the further stage of acting out how these holy people, who could not agree on earth, would get on in Heaven. One of the Cumming girls had the last line – 'In my Father's House are many mansions'.

CHAPTER 5

AGED FOURTEEN AND
A LITTLE LATER

Our house-move from Torran to Oscaig was precipitated by the continuing attitude of part of the congregation who held the view that if the Mission House was available then a lay preacher would be found and the church would be once more the area of focal and vocal interest. This materialistic approach to spiritual matters could not be reconciled and the Mission House remained unoccupied for some forty years. It has since been given a face-lift. The exterior walls have been 'picked' and the local stone, dressed by the builders, has aesthetic appeal and blends in with the countryside.

The local population dwindled at a fast rate and the school closed many years ago. The building comprising the school and the dwelling house was purchased by a Raasay man, but he did not choose to live there and one can only conclude that he regarded his purchase as an investment. It is a solid building on a firm found but the passing years have taken their toll and renovation is overdue.

Another factor which influenced our move was, I suspect, the continuing courting by my father of our future step-mother. Oscaig is only one and a half miles from Clachan – an invigorating walk by country standards. My father possessed a gun, which used gunpowder and had a ram-rod – a muzzle loader. I was not alone in thinking that he did not care much about shooting rabbits which had proliferated around Oscaig, but anyway, it was a good excuse for disappearing for a couple of hours of an evening. It did not take us long to find out that much about the same time as he was on his way, the lady from Clachan was on her way to the 'Orchard' which lay in deep woodland, halfway to Oscaig but by a different route. There were excellent brambles by the inshore loch, and if these were out of season kindlings had to be collected, or perhaps fresh moss for the flower pots. There was no shortage of acceptable excuses for being deep in the woods. What eventually happened to the gun I know not, but by now it would have been a museum piece. Digressing somewhat, the hardware, both in and out of doors, that was then in use, now belongs to a past age. Some of it may be found highly priced in antique shops, but many crofters threw away brass and cast-iron utensils and implements, not to mention the beautiful ewer sets, and also the oval style tureens and vegetable dishes which always adorned the kitchen dressers or 'shelf' to be found in most croft-house kitchens.

The move from Torran generated the usual excitement that occurs on such occasions. In our case, it was probably set at a higher pitch, bearing in mind that we were at an impressionable age. Furniture, goods and chattels went by boat, courtesy of the *Fladda Maid*. Murdo, now eighteen, and Trochan were in charge of the cattle and they had a long twelve-mile trek on a very hot day in May. Aunt Mary, my brother Torquil, my sister and I, together with our two cats – Daisy and Blackie – had the benefit of a motor car from Brochel Castle. Daisy disappeared within days and found her way back to Torran where I retrieved her during the school (summer) holiday. Her life in the rough must have taught her a sharp lesson, as she wandered no more, other than to meet 'Tom' and occasionally catch a rabbit which she carried proudly back home in appreciation, as it were, of the considerations shown to her.

Cats are possessive animals. On one occasion our cat had two pretty kittens. They were fluffy and in consequence we handled them far too much for their mother's liking. One morning, on entry into the barn where pussy had her box, my sister was horrified to find both kittens decapitated. Aunt Mary told us that she had seen a weasel about but she knew and we knew later that it was the work of the mother cat. I have to admit that we gave Trochan more than a passing look. He somehow had landed himself over the years the odd job of cat and dog disposer. The procedure was quite simple. Surplus kittens and puppies were placed in a sack with a large stone for company and then consigned to the deep. The favourite disposal spot, always at high tide, was from a rock directly below our house in Torran known as 'the Lewisman's Laimrig'. This part of the foreshore has some historical significance and obviously refers to a certain person from Lewis. The Gaelic word *Laimrig* is descriptive of the part of the foreshore between the points of anchorage and landing. Older dogs and cats did not escape this ultimate fate either. A dog throwing a fit was dispatched in this way without further ado, despite the time and effort needed to train another, far less the consideration of bonds of affection which are often associated with humans and domesticated animals, particularly dogs.

On another occasion, Aunt Mary went off on a Thursday for a few days' holiday, by way of attending a communion weekend in the south end of Raasay. Bellag Handy, the post lady, delivered a parcel on the following day, addressed to my father. It was a most unusual occurrence at that time of year. A piece of paper inside the parcel said 'From Maggie'. We assumed she was an older cousin who had been kind to us over the years. We knew that she had a housekeeper's post in Portree and although the Raasay postmark puzzled us, we were far more interested in the good things which the parcel contained. It was a veritable food hamper, including cake, sweets, fruit and about two pounds of sliced bacon. Our benefactor was of course none other than our future step-mother, Peggy (Maggie and Peggy identify the same fore-name). My father, with a twinkle in his eyes, let us draw our own conclusions, gave us sweets and placed the groceries in the kitchen dresser cupboard, other than the 'Ayrshire' bacon – for breakfast on the Sabbath day – which he placed between two large plates on the top shelf, which, like the lower one, ran all but the full length of the wooden partition between the staircase and the kitchen cum living room. The top shelf protruded slightly further than the lower one and was also a little longer at each end. As in most crofters' kitchens, they were loaded with a display of dishes and other knick-knacks gifted over the years. The dishes, incidentally, were repositories for string, boot laces, safety pins, hairpins and many other small articles needing a home. My father made due preparation for breakfast on Sunday morning. The big cast-iron frying pan was ready and there was great excitement – after all, a bacon and egg breakfast was a special treat. My father, having by now removed the plates which he had so carefully placed on the top shelf the previous Friday, could only stare in disbelief – no more than three rashers of bacon left! Where had all the bacon gone? There was only one possibility – the cat must have taken it! We had to make do with fresh fried fish again while Trochan had the last of the bacon. He also had poor pussy and she landed at the bottom of Loch Arnish early next day, despite my own and my sister's pleas. Our uncle was not an easy man to live with at the best of times, and I think that my father gave him a bacon breakfast just in case he should commit cat murder on the Sabbath!

We could not bring ourselves to tell our father about the bacon barbecue that we had shared the previous evening with our cousins over the hill, whilst he was busy fishing from the rocks in Arnish. The consequences were dramatic and we would not have shed a tear had Trochan landed at the bottom of Loch Arnish instead of pussy. I related the incident to my father and stepmother, many years later. Even then, with the passage of time adding its mellowing flavour to earlier feelings, father made no comment but Peggy (Maggie) had a good laugh.

Oscaig differs from Torran in many ways. Even the very stones are different. Torran has rock that is predominantly red, but all around Oscaig it is an uninteresting brown and grey with considerable slag like the left-overs of an earth eruption, which probably they are. Geography lessons had taught us over the past years that Raasay is diverse, ecologically. It is a dream island for geologists, botanists and other naturalists. The variety of rock – sandstone, limestone, granite and gneiss being some prime examples – had an effect on the distribution of both plant and animal life. Torran and the rest of the north end of Raasay had good patches of natural woodland and the brooks or streams that interspersed the hillsides added to the natural beauty of the countryside. Oscaig had little to offer by way of bushes and there was far less verdure than in Torran. It was also distinctly colder, catching as it does the sharp shafts of the north wind. On the credit side, Oscaig had good arable crofts, albeit small ones. Most of them nowadays seem to be out-run. There was a sizeable extension of common grazing. Most of the Oscaig crofters also had the benefit of some three acres of extension to arable land nearby, either because of holding a share in the Clubstock or as a temporary extension granted by the landlord, the Department of Agriculture for Scotland. As in Torran, we were still beside the seaside. The original six croft-houses form a pleasing crescent, each one within hailing distance but far enough away to afford as much or as little privacy as anyone may wish. The ranch-style bungalows were built, each to house two fatherless families, during the period when Raasay was owned by the

'Wood' family. Over the old deer fence in Oscaig lies 'Manitoba' where a row of derelict terraced houses, also built for widows, may still be seen. The ruins make useful fanks but it does seem a pity that tragedy and comedy reflected in memories of bygone days are lost forever. Oscaig Lodge, situated on higher ground beside the old deer fence, has a commanding view of the sea and the Isle of Skye.

Shortly after we settled in Oscaig, the widowed tenant of the lodge, who used to live in Glasgow until the start of the war, took up permanent residence. (The area must have had an attraction for widows.) She was an eccentric old dear who could be seen at first light, attired in her nightgown and posh slippers, tending the rockery in front of her living-room window. After I joined the Merchant Navy, I met her in Kyle of Lochalsh one cold and crisp morning. She was off to Glasgow and I was rejoining my ship in Scapa Flow. She was delighted to join me for tea in the upstairs tearoom of the Waverley Hotel. The owner, Mrs Stewart, produced a pot of good tea and a cakestand generously loaded with scones, pancakes and other confections, which at that time were in short supply. I, full of myself at the tender age of eighteen, was proud to pay the bill! Mrs Stewart made a quick assessment of the cost of the food consumed and charged something in the region of one shilling and six-pence each. With nothing less in my pocket than a ten shilling note, the hard pressed woman had to go downstairs for change. My elderly lady companion, shocked at what she considered to be an exorbitant cost, scooped what was left of the teabread into a rather large handbag. I, mortified and in deep shock at the turn of events, stood between the empty cakestand and Mrs Stewart on her return, gave her a handsome tip of one shilling, and beat a hasty retreat down the stair, followed by the lady of the lodge, to whom I said a quick goodbye and walked very quickly indeed to the station. Later, much later, as I boarded the naval night train,

Jellicoe, in Perth, bound for Thurso, I still had a picture in my mind of the look on Mrs Stewart's face when the cakestand came into view and I fled the room. There was also in my mind a picture of the procurer of pastries, with sheer shock showing in her wrinkles at what she genuinely considered a 'rip off'. We were charged only against what we had eaten and the charge was reasonable. She genuinely believed that it had all been paid for and was ours to take. Well, I paid and she took. There was no food on the train. Pangs of hunger by the time we reached Perth helped to relive the events of the morning, and left me thinking that a handbag had its uses. Doggie bags came much later! Everything is relative and who can judge senses of values!

There was an attitude towards land rights in Oscaig – something rather different from what we had experienced in Torran. If our cattle strayed on to some neighbour's croft, even when not under cultivation, the dog as like as not would be used to chase them off. The action was precipitate but without malice – just a way of life. During our first few months in our new home, in an endeavour to improve the house surroundings, I cut some turf about one hundred yards above the house. An outspoken female descended on me, like a ship in full sail, and harangued me for interfering with the common grazing. I was made to feel like a naughty schoolboy caught out but was prompted to rejoin that there was plenty of soil and she would untimately only have six feet of it all to herself. She was, for once, shocked into silence, threatened to tell my father but didn't, and we got on famously ever after. Later in life I learnt much more about common grazing, the Land Court, the Board of Agriculture for Scotland, landlords and crofters' security of tenure. In hindsight it was not difficult to identify the reasons for land protection by crofters. The generation to which my female neighbour belonged knew all about evictions and Highland Clearances and there was a natural in-built defence mechanism.

155

The south end of Raasay had much more to offer adolescents than Torran. This was how it seemed at the time, but decades later I am not too sure. Oscaig, with its lodge, deer fence and shore storehouse still had the marks of private ownership in 1939. There were good stone walls used as land boundaries, complete with large iron gates. The everlasting iron bed-end doing duty as a gate could be seen here and there, and Lilian Beckwith has made the most of that one! Islanders are not cheese-paring but they have had to take the rough with the smooth – the rough more often than not – over many centuries. They find a use for everything and recycling is just a swish expression in conservation and development programmes. Cattle grids came to stay and this indeed was progress.

It was an interesting and happy part of my life. There was the novelty of a new home, new school and new neighbours. Uncle Ewen – my mother's brother – and his family had moved into the croft-house next door. The tailor, father of the Maclean 'scholars', had lived there for many years and many a budding apprentice had cut cloth in the little outhouse which did duty as a shop. The house remained empty for some time and was in need of repair. Uncle Ewen had previously lived in Balachurn about two miles to the north of Oscaig, in the family home where my own mother was born. It laid claim to three crofts and is at the bottom of a deep glen – more of a ravine. Two of the houses, built under towering rocks, enjoy little sun. The loch at the bottom of the glen is dank and uninviting. It is a part of Raasay which looks well in pictures but for which I do not care. Meeting the charming people who live there is one of the few pleasures that may be derived from a visit. As a bonus, one may gaze across the loch towards Balmeanach which is on high ground with heathery moorland for background and catches a fair amount of sun.

We did not know Uncle Ewen and his family too well

previously, so with our added interest in his house repair, we made up for lost time. He had spent some time in America, farming with Uncle Calum, his brother, and we had it in our minds that he was rich. It may well have been so had he not been so soft-hearted and kind. He had a cross-cut saw which contributed to an easier workload and improved the community spirit for firewood collection, especially when the Forestry Officer (the shoemaker) was not looking! Uncle Ewen owned no fewer than two horses and accoutrements such as a cart, plough and harrow, also a small boat. No wonder we, in our simplicity, thought he was rich! His oldest son, Torquil, was the ploughman and I can remember the joy of seeing for the first time the long dark brown furrows of ploughed patches on our croft (with the seagulls making short work of the worms) and the feeling that having Torquil as a neighbour signalled the end of the *cas chrom* era. What a versatile piece of equipment – the plough! It was used not only for planting our Kerr's Pinks and Golden Wonders, but for lifting them as well – progress indeed! I can still recall that one creel of seed potatoes produced nine on the Oscaig Park extension to our croft, and this without the massive application of red and black seaweed, as was the case in Torran. Seed potatoes of course meant that the pieces with 'eyes' (sprouts) were cut out of the potato and used for planting. The sterile parts were kept for the bill of fare. There was no point in burying a whole potato, especially at the time of year when the stock was running low. There was also less for the insatiable crows!

The ploughman homeward plods his weary way
And leaves the world to darkness and to me.

The application of such an elegy was not for us. Life was black and white without any grey! Torquil ploughed on, single and footloose. The Maginot Line seemed secure. There was plenty of life around us with the influx of

157

evacuees, and in our insularity and adolescence I could see no cause to express any sorrowful sentiment as Torquil continued with his ploughing, providing us with a comfortable croft life.

With the advent of tractors, the two horses, Polly and Bess, were put to grass or declared 'redundant'. I do not know how they ended their days, but meat was rationed at that time and their demise may have been in keeping with the Raasay tradition relating to the 'Cow-Horse' (*Each Mart*). Skye folk, in particular, have maintained over the years that in their ignorance raw Raasay ranchers made a bovine mistake and ate a horse. It had often occurred to me that Uncle Ewen, who lived on to his mid-nineties, liked spare ribs.

Uncle Ewen's son Donald, some six years older than me, had been a steward in David Macbrayne's most prestigious ship the *Loch Garry* and latterly in the *Loch Ness,* which for many years was on the Stornoway, Applecross, Kyle of Lochalsh, Armadale and Mallaig run. He gained considerable experience about the Lewis way of life, *bothans*, *gugachan* and *caithris na h-oidhche* in particular (illicit drinking dens, salted young solan geese and 'bundling' in that order). He was nicknamed 'Sailor' and the picture that he painted of life on the ocean wave – Stornoway, after all, was a long way off – fired my imagination and planted the seeds of a career at sea in my mind, albeit they took some little while to germinate! He was at home during the autumn and winter of 1939, making himself both useful and a nuisance about the house while awaiting his call-up papers. He was good at playing draughts but practice makes perfection, well nearly, and he did not by any means always get his own way, once I got the measure of his moves. We joined in many a game during the winter evenings, mostly in our house, as it was warmer with its thick wooden floor which had been acquired as flotsam – the result of a ship's cargo of wood

158

being ditched in heavy weather some years previously. 'It's an ill wind . . .' The heat and light from the tilley lamp added to the cosiness of the household scene.

When we fancied a change of venue, we landed of an evening in Susan's house which was a few hundreds yards up the road. Susan was a character, in a class of her own. When she came to Raasay as a bride, previously widowed, she had to put up with the indignity of living in a storehouse by the shore, some two miles from Oscaig, until the new home was built. Having previously lived in Clydebank she knew about the better things of life, and on first sight of her shore haven after landing in Raasay, she was reputed to have said loudly, 'You're now buggered for life, Susan Macnair' (her previous name). This declaration naturally set a few locals talking – such language indeed. The woman could neither speak nor understand Gaelic and felt at a disadvantage from the outset; but Susan was made of sterner stuff and before long she was to be seen on the scaffolding with her husband busily building their new home, which they duly completed – with 'mod cons'. The water system had shortcomings over the years, some said short pipes, but the system was there in principle if not always in practice. Much the same could be said in our own day when it comes to 'a systematic approach to getting things done'. She liked her food and her comfort. Draughts from the back scullery were quickly overcome by using her husband Angus's hill clothing for door draught excluders. At this time he was working as an electrician in Glasgow, where it was rumoured some residents had experienced shock tremors long before the German air raids.

We spent happy evenings with Susan. The favourite card game was 'Catch the Ten'. Bella, an evacuee neighbour, and cousin Katie, who both had to get along without their husbands for a season, often joined the card school. They made the tea and handed round the scones. Susan, who waddled at the best of times, was short and tubby, and once

159

ensconced in her barrel chair was happy to stay there and continue with the card game which she took seriously, but no money changed hands. She enjoyed the service provided and the hilarity which Bella and Katie never failed to generate, made her evening. It was a new experience for me to see women smoke. Woodbine, Craven A and Gold Flake were the popular brands. The anecdote may seem simple and of little significance in an age of television, video and fast-changing values, but it was a way of life which was personalised and the relationship strengthened bonds of caring and friendship. Happy days!

Years later, by which time Susan had television and was nearer ninety than eighty, she took to dressing up for her choice programmes so that those appearing on the screen could see her in her finery. When we went to live in Oscaig the countryside was clean. Uncle Murdo, who lived in Inverarish, in one of sixty-four two-roomed houses, built for miners, kept the ground and paths around Raasay House in first class order. There were only three motor cars on the island, including Kenny's post office van. The first stage of environmental defilement resulted from the iron ore mining activity which started and developed in the second decade of this century. The kilns, powerhouses and other edifices remained for many years after their work was finished – the kilns sticking out like crude phallic symbols, impotent and vulgar in their despoiled surroundings. Some will argue that the project brought island improvements; others will disagree.

The well-built pier is a legacy from those days. It is in a very exposed position and has been cursed by many – some under their breath – when the steamer failed to call, often in the teeth of a south-west gale. Indeed, although it was not for want of trying, it passed by in prevailing conditions as related, during the evening before my own wedding in Portree, leaving my father, sister and best man (who else but

Torquil next door) as well as the groom to exchange looks of disbelief. I did not curse – I cannot speak for the others – but my sister fell back on a woman's traditional reserve and cried. All was well the following morning. We took an 'Irishman's journey', south to go north, and made it to the church not a moment too soon as the minister had all but given up hope of seeing us and was preparing for a burial service for which his church had been booked that very day.

We returned to Raasay House which was then the hotel, where we had the wedding breakfast and a first-class Highland wedding reception. We were ferried across from Portree to Raasay in a large fishing boat in the darkest of dusk on a December evening with the wind running high. The boat was crewed by fishermen friends of my father who made the most of the occasion – but all that is another story!

Despite local fears and criticism over the years and an apparent despotic selfishness exercised by the owner of property and land in Raasay at that time, the pier provided some mooring facilities for the car ferry which gives a regular weekday service – with severe fares – between Raasay and Sconser, each terminal now complete with good slipways, and relief facilities by way of a super loo.

The second stage of environmental defilement which affected the ecology can be attributed to the tree-felling and saw-mill operations that accelerated as the war developed. The state of the countryside went from bad to worse, and by the mid-70s, it was nothing short of painful to all who could recall better days. Cars, mostly second-hand, came to Raasay in fair number, and after some more years' service ended up as unsightly scrap all over the place.

Old Charlie from Suishnish had quite a good car but it had arguments with various land fixtures and ended up as a hen-house. Unsightly outhouses, many made of timber 'seconds', popped up in profusion in Inverarish. The residents there, even at this time, could not claim a prize for the

161

best kept private housing estate. The gardens run parallel to the road and many of them ooze neglect. This is a pity as the soil is good and could be worked with ease. Few gardens sport a border of flowers. There are, to be fair, some residents who do have pleasing home surroundings. A number of owners use the houses merely as holiday homes.

The provision of a refuse dump and the subsequent regular collection of household refuse has now gone a long way towards a much needed improvement of the surroundings, and all who helped to bring about this change are to be congratulated. The land adjacent to Raasay House and the farm had been an eyesore for years, with the clock tower on the farm-steading a mere monument to its past glory. The story goes that the clock, whose chimes could be heard in Braes, Skye, went 'off strike' at the beginning of the First World War when local lads left to join up. No amount of persuasion from time-served engineers could get it to go 'on strike' ever after. The whole clock mechanism came out in sympathy. All that remained was a skeleton without even a key.

With a new administration the area around Raasay House has been given a face-lift and may yet have some of its past dignity restored. The large garden, complete with hothouses at the back of the hotel and the orchard about a mile uphill, belonged to another age when all kinds of vegetables, luscious fruit and flowers appeared, each in its own season. The gardener's cottage, whitewashed and trim, offered us a passing invitation on our way home from school, in the person of the gardener's widowed mother, who met us unfailingly with thick slices of bread and home-made jam (pieces). She could not have been well off but such a consideration would not have crossed her mind. She would have parted with her last slice of loaf in return for the appreciation which we were no doubt ready to show. Kenneth, her son, was a hard worker and a good gardener.

His command of English could have been better and grammar was firmly on the list of his imperfections. Showing some lady visitors round the garden, and coming to a fine display of wallflower, he was heard to remark conversationally, 'She is no good in the bed but all right against the wall'. Perhaps it was a rambling rose!

'Send no meat – I am killing myself tonight' was the terse message that the local butcher received from Kenneth on another occasion. The story, allowing for grammatical inexactitudes, reveals that in those days Raasay had a butcher's shop. It has long since gone and no one in Raasay seems inclined to invest in a butcher's business. The shop – the only one in Raasay – with somewhat limited stock, does its best to meet customers' meat requirements if they order in advance. Such is progress.

Raasay House had become an hotel by the time I moved to Oscaig. It was licensed to sell drink, despite protests and petitions, and seasonal bookings had been established by the time war broke out. Raasay became part of a declared 'protected area', and as a result the business life of the hotel came to a virtual standstill. There were the occasional local weddings, children's Christmas parties, a few whist drives and dancing classes. All of these activities provided first-class material for the preacher's sermons. He seemed to be well informed about the goings on. We had our own suspicions, and the suspected source of his information was well provided with vivid descriptions and lurid details of an evening's non-event.

I was a tall strapping and, some said, good looking lad in my sixteenth year. Susan, who lived up the road in Oscaig Park corner house, grabbed me as her escort for the hotel dancing classes and whist drives. She was a roly-poly of a woman even then well in her 60s, but was she not light on her feet! Her Clydebank accent was most pronounced when she was displeased with her husband Angus – a regular event.

The dancing always finished in good time, and having seen Susan home, I too was indoors at a respectable hour, as all 16-year-olds should, heard the book being read, and was soon fast asleep in the tranquillity which Oscaig provided.

I cannot help but reflect on the double standards that prevailed at that time among those who should have known better. Grown men went to great lengths to get to and from the hotel bar undetected. Talk about 'taking the low road'! That was precisely what they did. Youngsters of my own age, lithe and lightfooted, played checkpoint games along the footpath by the shore. A surprising number of folk could be seen equipped for rock fishing or shooting, taking a detour through the hotel grounds which rolled down towards Clachan bay. They were noticeably unsuccessful in finding fish, fowl or furries. These antics caused no end of amusement for some of the 'open' regulars, like Kenny the Post who made no secret of his liking for a half and a half pint. It was even better when someone else 'stood his hand'.

The press, always ready to sniff a story, made the most of an allegation, shortly after the hotel opened with a drinks licence, that many who attended local funerals found their way to the hotel bar. I recall vividly the sensation that this disclosure created at the time with denial and counter-denial. What really was there to deny! With one cemetery on the hotel doorstep for all the distance between them, and the other over a nearby hilltop, those who carried the bier in all seasons deserved a beer – a case of keeping awake so to speak!

The first formal function that I attended in the hotel was in November 1940, for the wedding of cousin Mary-Anne. In contrast to the practice in England, where weddings take place either in a church or in a registrar's office, normally before three o'clock in the afternoon, four o'clock at the latest, no such restrictions apply in Scotland. Weddings take place quite often in the evening and the knot is tied in an hotel. This is a very convenient and stylish arrangement as the guests walk straight into the reception afterwards. On their way out later – much later – they do not perhaps walk quite so straight. The arrangement is also more comfortable in cold weather than being in a church which invariably is cold. The seats and hotel surroundings in general also have greater appeal.

The bride looked radiant, so everyone said in so many words, and the wedding breakfast provided by Mrs Davidson, the hotel proprietor, was very good indeed. I still recall that we started off with a wholesome broth, with chicken for the main course. The sweet was light, frothy and pink. What a marvellous dessert – everyone said it was Kate the cook's special recipe. Derek Cooper's contribution to the culinary art came much later. 'It is called a bavaroyce (bavarois) but I myself like farola,' proclaimed Peigi Bheag (little Peggy) loudly, for all and sundry to hear. Her command of English was not good but she had held court in Glasgow, as the wife of a police inspector, and knew all about fancy dishes. She was a great girl was Peggy. Johnny Phadruig (John the son of Patrick or Peter) the local shop-keeper, to whom reference has been made in another chapter, was a respected older member of the community and he made a witty speech which was well received. After the meal was over, he kissed the bride and went home.

The social side of the evening with some help from Messrs Haig, Walker, Dewar and Usher, was swinging along nicely. Cousin Torquil and my father were in fine form, as was Alasdair Fhionnlaigh (Alasdair the son of Finlay). About ten o'clock, which was early as weddings go in the islands, a cryptic message was received to say that Johnny Phadruig had died suddenly. Cousin Torquil told my father.

'What did you say, Torquil?'

'We have just heard that Johnny Phadruig has just died in his chair.'

'What,' said my father, 'is it for good?'

'Well,' chipped in Alasdair, 'whatever he did, he has spoilt a good night for us.'

It would have been disrespectful for the function to continue, and the guests dispersed in near silence. It was certainly one occasion when the bride and groom were able to reach the bedchamber without interruption. The bad news could have waited until the morning but there always has to be a spoil-sport.

When I was a little older, in September 1942, to be precise, my own father had his wedding reception in Raasay House Hotel – 'like father, like son'. It was of course his second time round and my legitimacy is secure. It was a great evening, following the actual wedding ceremony in Portree in the early afternoon. The wedding party went by the *Loch Ness* from Raasay to Kyle, by ferry to Kyleakin and then by car to Portree. Fortified by cups of tea and a dram in the Portree Hotel, it was time for the return journey. My brother, Murdo (Luli), then twenty-one, was enjoying himself by late evening, and my father felt it prudent to suggest to him that he take things a little easier and pointed to me as a good behavioural example. At that stage of the proceedings, my father lost his balance and toppled over the nearest settee straight into the lap of a well-known local old maid, who it was said was good with her hands and knew a thing or two about the male anatomy. My stepmother glowered momentarily, continued in fine fettle and the situation was soon retrieved.

The youngsters did their stuff and apart from the bridal apple pie bed, the trussed live cockerel between the sheets had to be disposed of before there was any question of 'afters'. My father was then sixty-six years of age but very active, like many of his generation. There was some aphrodisiac in their diet about which they probably knew nothing – if they did, they kept it to themselves, but no-one grew or ate celery. The cockerel at least escaped the fate of his predecessors. Had he been black and lived not so many years earlier, he would most surely have been buried alive as a cure for epilepsy – an ailment from which during adolescence my brother Torquil was a victim.

The hotel was a convivial and pleasant place for social gatherings in those days. It was furnished beautifully and had a distinctive elegance and style of its own. The library with its panelled walls and large stock of leather-bound books had to be seen to be believed – a veritable haven for any human 'worm'. The exterior of the building was also in good order. Sadly, this historical building with its lawns and meadows rolling to the seashore, about which so much has been written, was allowed to decay over the years. No-one with an appreciation of practicalities can anticipate a return to its former glory, short of a sheik showing a shekel. Had Borrodale House not been renovated and converted into an hotel in 1981, matters might have been different. Much has been written about the uncaring attitude of Dr Green who owned the hotel and other property on Raasay. He was known locally and further afield as 'Doctor No' simply because he seemed to say 'no' to any proposals for improvement. His long absence from Raasay was ample evidence of his lack of appreciation of local sensitivity and of what the island had to offer. More in sorrow than in anger one is prompted to suggest that although the continued neglect of Raasay House was in itself an act of vandalism, it was not the only act of vandalism. Dr Green did not break the windows, smash crockery, scatter bedding all over the place and remove goods of substance and chattels. Those who had nothing better to do must also have had difficulty in distinguishing between their own property and that of others. Someone somewhere must know who the trespassers and guilty parties were. It was plain thievery. If the carved lions which overlook the one-time hotel from the old pier could see and speak, there might be a few revelations in store.

The Highlands and Islands Development Board took over the property in the late 70s and leased part of it to the Scottish Adventure School Trust who made a genuine effort to renovate parts of the building. The School Trust, under able direction, seems to have had a wide discretion in carrying out repair work, but its resources were not without limit. With hindsight, it may have been a better financial proposition had the new landlord, the Highlands and Islands Development Board, concentrated on the re-conversion of the building to an hotel. Such a sentiment may be no more than conjecture, but the beautiful building with its historical halo – the ancient seat of the Macleods of Raasay – will be a talking point for years to come. Whatever the future holds, it is good to know that the unhappy saga of Raasay House at least provided occupational therapy for young people less privileged than I was as a boy, although some of us who can recall the earlier years of elegance may feel saddened on seeing a surfeit of plasterboard where once polished panels mirrored the surroundings. It is my own hope that part of the building will continue as a permanent community centre on the island. Who knows – this grand old house may yet regain a measure of its former dignity. There is no harm in dreaming dreams and being an optimist!

Following the era of the School Trust, most of the building became an Outdoor Centre, providing at modest rates accommodation and food, an indoor games area, a camping site, equipment for hire, including transport, climbing, abseiling, canoeing, wind-surfing, sailing and guided walks.

By 1940 the sizeable plantation of trees came under the axe and the war years saw great activity with a saw-mill producing precious props, planks and plenty of firewood. The Creagan Beag (Small Rocks) within sight of Oscaig were laid bare and the desolate look on the hillsides lacked appeal. Thankfully, the area was replanted and, at the time of writing, the trees are truly a coniferous plantation. The overall 'scenery' still does not compare with the natural beauty provided by the Torran habitat, with the random growth of birch, hazel, willow and mountain ash – all on a woodland carpet of wild grass and moss with an ever-changing floral pattern of primrose, bluebell, daisy, butter-cup, celandine, violet, dandelion and marsh marigold, and a raised pattern of foxglove, fern, catkin and the wild rose. The foregoing is but a sample! True it is that the thick clusters of rhododendron provide colour and a beauty of their own along the roadside between Oscaig and Clachan and again on the way from Millpark towards Inverarish Cottages and the 'Glen'.

To our delight, wild strawberries were there for the picking at the Creagan Beag and there were plenty of raspberries for those of us in the know. Wending our way shorewards at ebb tide brought us the pleasure of collecting razorfish, perhaps better known as spoutfish. These were to be found in large pockets of sand at the bottom of Oscaig Park. The sun seemed to attract them and the gush of the brine which they 'expelled' was the signal for attack. Down went our wooden 'staves' at a pronounced angle – never perpendicular – and contact was made. A quick dig followed and it was all over for the spoutfish. We were not always successful and the shellfish, virtually within our grasp, disappeared at fantastic speed into the depth of the sand. Such is self-preservation and the tricks of nature. Well washed, to get rid of the sand which lodges inside the shell, then lightly simmered and seasoned, they provide a delect-able dish to be enjoyed by old and young alike.

Rock fishing was a favourite pastime at Meall Oscaig – a rocky promontory at the bottom of the crofts. There is a very steep drop into deep water, and we were discouraged at that stage in our lives from including it in our wanderings. Most of the shore which skirts Oscaig is to this day clean, with deep water, and I would accept scavenger fish such as mackerel on the menu, if I knew it had been caught off Oscaig. Some well-known rocks (*sgeirean*), nearly covered by neap tides, set the scene for excellent fishing. The Inner Minch has been trawled ruthlessly over many years and fish is now scarce – a near unbelievable phenomenon for those of us who can recall the time when fresh fish was taken for granted – all that was needed was the use of a boat, line or rod.

One happy memory is of setting off in the late sunset for Inver, down the west coast of Raasay, in Uncle Ewen's boat, which he was happy to share with us – a true philanthropist was Uncle Ewen. I was the youngest of the crew which also included my father, Uncle Ewen and his son Torquil, who in later years married my wife's sister, fathered two of a family around his mid-century (he was fond of cream) and lived on in Oscaig. The boat, complete with an 'outboard' engine, must have been loaded past the 'plimsoll' line, with herring nets and victuals! The fishing lines were out and a fish supper was assured even before the nets were set. The boat was beached and a *bothan* (small hut) close by was soon made comfortable for our overnight stay. A large fire of sticks and driftwood provided warmth and the means to cook supper. Sleeping bags had not been heard of and we slept in our clothes with some extra overcoats for feet warmers. The fire was kept going overnight. Torquil snored so there was no need for an alarm clock. Refinements such as vacuum flasks were not even considered and I had morning tea brewing in the kettle by five o'clock, just as darkness was giving way to dawn. The nets were soon hauled and we were not disappointed with the catch. I cannot ever recall feeling cold on a fishing trip, but fishing with father was not my happiest of hobbies. He seemed not to have any fear of the sea and was at his happiest when the boat bounced and bobbed in a white crested sea and was in sail. It took me some time and a tumble backwards before I could reconcile the pull of my oar with the pull of the sea. Rowlocks, cleats, jibs and halyards were not for me – but I dreamt of big ships and travelling the world!

Nowadays, I cannot claim to get the call of the sea, and fishing is not one of my interests in life. It has nothing to do with my belief that fish suffer pain, contrary to my teacher's pronouncements that because fish are cold-blooded they feel no pain. It could be that, subconsciously, there is an element of fear on my part, following an experience some years ago, when I thought for sure that my sister-in-law, Torquil's wife Mary-Ann, stocky and stout, was on the point of capsizing the boat as she straddled the thwart seat – too much to starboard for my liking – and wrestled with her fishing tackle in cold blood. The fish, fortunately, got away, thus putting her contortions to a speedy end, and we made for port, 'steady as she goes'. I still like fish, including the pink variety, particularly if it is poached 'just for the pot'!

On leaving school I used to help my father with the maintenance of the 'New' Cemetery which is laid out on high ground above Clachan on one side and the 'Orchard' on the other with the Mill Loch skirting the wide path which leads to it. It was not easy to trim the graves, as they were mounded, but none were neglected. One part of the cemetery is walled off. The masonry was the work of crafts-men and I believe this section had been specially set aside for the 'Wood' family who had owned Raasay at one stage. They are not buried there but the names of two of the sons who were killed in the First World War are inscribed on the War Memorial at Suisnish. Another part of the cemetery had been used for the burial of German prisoners of war, and a very large stone marked their graves, complete with inscribed names.

The Second World War had brought its own emotions

but we tended these graves with the same care as was exercised with all the others. The remains have since been removed and re-interred in their last resting place in Germany. The stone, which had been manhandled from the shore to the cemetery by German prisoners of war (no mean feat as it was all uphill), was also removed from the cemetery and placed near the entrance gateway. It is a piece of history and one would hope that it might be preserved. There is now a sizeable extension to the cemetery but at the time of writing it does not have the aesthetic appearance of the original section.

One of the most pleasing aspects about Oscaig is its setting. There is a wonderful view from any angle – the sea – high tide and low tide – in all its moods, calm, in froth and in fury reflecting the murky clouds or the blue of the sky – the 'sea rocks' rugged and craggy as they appear to rise and all but sink in the ever-flowing tide – the gulls, watchful for a morsel, and the gannet in more active mood, taking a dive for dinner – the movement of sea craft, motorised, in sail or with oars – the Isle of Skye over the Sound of Raasay, with its lofty peaks in all their majesty whatever the season – Braes showing off their sloping pastures as they change colour to suit the seasons, dotted with crofters' cottages, gleaming white in sunshine and in storm. What could be more pleasant and invigorating than a fast stroll over the hilltops above Oscaig, with Creachan as the destination?

The sun offers a bonus in colour and vista but a cloudy sky with soft rain drizzling has a charm of its own whilst wind and heavy rain show off what nature has to offer in terms of bleak contrast. There was a path across the moor in my young days and it was well traversed, usually with the objective of rounding up the cattle for milking and their overnight keep. The rubbish dump which is at least situated in a deep dell at Creachan, is a recent innovation and, in fairness to the planners, does not spoil the view. A few hundred yards further on finds us at the one and only house, now used as a youth hostel. The view from here is panoramic and the peacefulness of the place is arresting. The mountain air, laced with the fragrance of flora and fauna, braces the senses and provides an aperitif beyond price.

Creachan House, during my teenage years, was the home of Somhairle Nicolson, grandfather of a much respected family, including Somhairle Maclean, the outstanding Gaelic bard, who, among his many other literary contributions, penned Gaelic verse using Raasay themes. A cairn complete with descriptive plaques was raised in his honour in 1988, at Hallaig, the setting of one of his most famous poems. Hallaig is also one of the sites from which crofters were evicted during the infamous 'Clearances'. The cairn also serves as a memorial to them. Somhairle's brother John also possessed outstanding literary talent. Students of Gaelic can enjoy a feast of the language in John's Gaelic translation of Homer's *Odyssey*. It is a splendid contribution to the Gaelic language. He prepared this work during his time as rector of Oban High School and it was published after his untimely death.

The Nicolsons at Creachan were charming and generous. Katie-Bella, an unmarried daughter, kept house and her brother Calum saw to the land husbandry. Later on, joined by their brother Angus, they took over the tenancy of Raasay Home Farm where they made a valuable contribution to community life and kept the farm steadings tidy and in good order.

The previous tenant of the home farm was a strange little man, known locally as 'Mighty'. He was also a far from pleasant character. His wife had a cowed, sad and timid look about her, and on our way to and from school we often heard him rave and rant at his farm hand, long before they came in sight. The language was choice. Curiosity aroused, we checked our dictionaries without success! The young lad, who had a welcome for everyone and was not afraid of doing a good day's work, suffered in silence. He also suffered the occasional clout which did not escape our notice; but had we not been taught to respect our seniors and not to tell tales? As a comparatively young man he landed in a mental hospital. Who can say what effect such physical and pyschological treatment may have had on him in his teenage and formative years? We on our part, feeling constrained and unhappy, found solace in all that nature had to offer around us, including Mighty's turnips!

As the summer days lengthened, our walks to Creachan, as often as not, continued. Conveniently we could see no cattle. The deep ravine to our right sheltered bird and beast, and sloping upwards some distance away, we could see the walled 'Orchard'. There, on more than one occasion, we heard Kate Macpherson, known locally as Kate Cumming – why, I know not – remonstrating with her husband outside the Orchard cottage in which they lived with five children. He was a character, not over-active and nicknamed 'An Ridire' (Sir): those people had style. Anyway, other than the echo of their voices nothing else imposed on the scene. Snooping youngsters were the soul of discretion and their immediate neighbours carried no tales. The cemetery was not quite within sight but well within earshot!

I can recall the splendour of wild flowers and fern as we wound our way past the Free Church grounds, complete with manse and where we celebrated the Coronation a few years previously, landing eventually at 'The Cottages'. These terraced houses were regarded as rather prestigious residences – the 'Milngavie' of the island. The houses are still there, and they are occupied, but the terraced building seems to have lost its pre-war superior appeal.

A hurried trot and we were in the shop by the shore. What luxury – a slab of toffee was ours for one penny and two large 'Skye' biscuits for another penny. We shared our money and we shared our procurements. A fast pace homewards by way of Clachan and the Creagan Beag helped our digestion. Other than a passing comment: 'What took you so long?', all was well. The wanderings of the cattle had covered our tracks. 'Trochan' set off in the direction of Balachurn to the north of Oscaig, for had we not already been to Creachan and found no cattle – at least not our own! On most occasions the cows made for home of their own accord and kept to the better road between Holman and Oscaig. They respected their hooves and were not so daft.

It was yet another instance which, on reflection, so often occurred to me, that crofters spend time doubling up on jobs or even creating them without an assessment of the prevailing circumstances. This determined effort to carry out a job for a job's sake appears a paradox and is not easy to reconcile to the traditional relaxed attitude of the crofter, so often wrongly interpreted as laziness. Even today in some island communities time is not all-important and the attitude to life is relaxed. Perhaps it is a trait which is held in common with the Spaniards from whom some islanders are without doubt descended. The Spaniards say 'we can do it tomorrow' (*mañana*). In the Hebrides, *'màireach'* (tomorrow) is a word that is often used. Tomorrow never comes, but the job in hand gets done with more regard to fair weather and foul, than to the element of time. The hue of the sky, the rainbow, the flight of feathers over the landscape, the nearness of the horizon and more than a passing look at the moon and the stars in the firmament, all, in their own way, tell the seasoned son of the soil what he needs to know and place the working pattern of life in perspective. *'Màireach'* may have a lesser sense of urgency than *'mañana'* – at least that is how Father Colin MacInnes of Barra interpreted it, according to a report by the 'Hon Man' in the *Sunday Post*.

Time waits for no one, it just passes you by –

Trying to keep up with time is a futile exercise. If a more relaxed approach to our respective ways of life could be cultivated, the world might be a better place for all of us during our relatively short sojourn on earth.

CHAPTER 6

A LITTLE LATER STILL

Boyhood days were behind me and I was in my adolescence. The war news, with the run-up to the fall of Dunkirk, was grave. Raasay had already suffered loss of life in battle and other young men were missing, including Uncle Donald's oldest son Murdo, who had joined the Queen's Own Cameron Highlanders some months before the start of the war. He was wounded and taken prisoner at St Valéry and the intervening period between the news that he was missing and confirmation that he was alive, was a time of tension for his parents, brothers and sister. It also rubbed off on us. We were close to cousin Murdo. He had started work as a mere lad, shepherding in Drumuie, near Portree. He intrigued us with his stories of life as a shepherd, living, as he did, week about in each of six croft houses! Russia could be taught a thing or two about a democratic community way of life. Murdo, on his return to Torran, never forgot to bring his younger cousins some chocolates, but my sister and I, in particular, liked him for his own sake. Great was our relief when we heard that he was safe.

September 1940 had us crowding round Susan's radio, elated with the news of air victories by the RAF. It was a very warm month with record crops, and everyone made a special effort to conserve, as the effects of rationing were by now being felt, even in country places. A cheerful young relation caught a rabbit, skinned it and insisted that Aunt Mary had it for the pot. Days later, one of his brothers was killed in action. Shortly afterwards he too was called up, contracted tuberculosis in the army and died. Why did some families have to suffer so much? It seemed so unreal when I reflected on the rabbit, but these were sad times and I was growing up in a world of change; the pace was faster and things would not ever be the same again. Insular as we were, compared with many places, no-one, even in the gloom which prevailed after news of Dunkirk, doubted Britain's ability to win the war. James Nicolson, Millplace, and other older men in Raasay who were past an age for active service, were great propagandists and young people such as myself were uplifted and impressed when they went into detail about Britain's prowess and the latest news, which always ended up with warm words for Mr Churchill. It was as though our elders, who had experienced the horrors of the First World War, were doing their best to reassure us that all would yet be well. Bombs rained on Britain's cities, ships were sunk ,and there must have been moments when they had doubts, but if so, they gave nothing away. Cousins, neighbours and chums, male and female, were by now part of the war movement. They came home on leave and left again – some to return no more.

They were born in humble homes with a background of bens for their castles. As they traversed the paths and the glens and skipped over the bogs and streams in their native island, no cares beset them. The humble sparrows, the strutting cockerels, the cackling hens, sheep bleating by the foreshore, cattle dreamily grazing in postage-stamp patches of fresh spring grass, tipped with dew, cats clawing at the bark of birch saplings and dogs at heel – all shared with them fresh Highland air and they breathed it freely. As they grew older, they lazed in purple and rusty beds of heather, or perched themselves on a stony dyke – a memorial to their forefathers – when the day's work was done. Their pleasures were simple. Life still had few cares.

178

The clouds gathered. Peals of thunder reverberated among the hills. The rain came, refreshing fields and foliage. The sun shone; Duncaan and the far off Cuillins glistened, enveloped in cloaks of purple and majestic in their splendour. The sky cleared and life went on, refreshed by cool breezes with a south-west drift.

But the clouds of war gathered and 'man's inhumanity to man' was reflected in the storm that followed. It wrought havoc in countless homes. The glens and outposts of the islands answered yet again the call of war. Many lives were sacrificed on the altar of avarice. There was despair, but there was hope. The storm was over but they would not return to cheer the hearth:

> Our Island youth from straths and glens marched by
> Seeking no claim to immortality.
> Their lives were taken; we live on to sigh –
> To cherish and respect their memory.

Miss Tallach, the school headmistress, extended a welcome to all from Raasay who were serving on land, sea and in the air, and gave each person a Bible with her own handwritten inscription. Mine, presented in due course, was inscribed 'Remember thy Creator in the days of thy youth'. I still have that Bible.

I was in my sixteenth year and restless. My brother had failed his 'call-up' medical examination owing to defective vision and was by now working in the British Aluminium Factory at Kinlochleven. Cousin Donald next door was in the army – destined for Burma – and I was fidgeting to fly away from the home nest, by no means an unusual occurrence with island youngsters. I could not get 'on my bike' as I did not have one! My chance came in June 1941 when, with many reservations by Aunt Mary, I accepted a job on Kenknock Farm, Glenlochay, Perthshire.

Before leaving home I visited a number of relations and

friends as was the established custom. When it came to say goodbye, I found tenshilling notes and half-crown pieces being placed in the palm of my hand. Although most acceptable, it was somewhat embarrassing as it was unthinkable to leave home for the first time without making these calls. As is so often the case, it was those with the least who gave the most. It was a touching experience. The practice is probably no more, due as much to these social calls not being made as it is to other social and economic changes in a way of life.

My departure from Raasay, accompanied by my father, was by rowing boat to Sconser where we stayed overnight. The charge for bed, breakfast and a cup of tea on arrival in the late evening, was two shillings each. In the early morning we went by bus to Armadale and then by David MacBrayne's 'steamer' to Mallaig where my father had a dram, gave me good advice and saw me on to the train. It was my first time on a bus, a steamer and a train – and all in one day! Torran schooldays came flooding back and I thought of Nelly's railway memory lessons, which we had found so dull. Was the train which I was about to board LMS or LNER? I knew it could not be GWR! I settled, rightly, for LNER. Nationalisation and British Rail had not yet arrived.

I did not care much for Mallaig with its pronounced fishy smells and hordes of seagulls hovering too close for comfort. The train left on time and the third-class carriage was comfortable. My impressions of Mallaig were soon forgotten as before me opened up the vista provided by Morar, Lochailort and Glenfinnan. The story had gone about that some whippets had been found yelping on Glenfinnan Station and that at one end of the station, a pair of boots could be seen moving under a massive pile of herring that had disgorged by accident from a railway track. Someone had said that the stationmaster was inside them and that he owned the whippets who liked herring on a smaller scale! On this occasion the fish must have stayed in Mallaig and all was quiet.

There was some delay at Fort William where I had the strange experience of the train shunting somewhere and seemingly going in reverse to get into the station! My brother came up from Kinlochleven to meet me and he slipped me a pound note. A German plane was reported to have buzzed Fort William during the night and the chatter was considerable. It was all rather exciting. I checked and – yes – I did have my gas mask, a standard government rubber issue in a cheap cardboard box. Other free rubber issues came later when I went to sea!

The train chugged on. The viaduct at Tyndrum caught my eye, and at one stage the engine and carriages in movement were all but in a half circle. It seemed to me like one of the seven wonders of the world. I had my head well out the corridor window and my father's advice went unheeded. Down below – a long way down below – a large house stood in splendid isolation in an extensive clearing among a plantation of conifers. I disembarked at Crianlarich where I was met by the farm manager – yet another cousin – Murdo. Descriptions of looks and what each would be wearing had been exchanged as we had not met previously. He was a pleasant person but rather deaf and in consequence our conversation was stifled. We boarded another train at Upper Crianlarich. These were the days – two railway stations in Crianlarich. It was indeed the age of the train!

The evening was warm and the car ride from Killin Junction to Kenknock Farm was bumpily pleasant. Murdo's mother (Aunt Johan) was the houskeeper. I had not met her before either but she welcomed me as she would any of her own five sons. The living room which was also the dining room and kitchen and which everyone shared, had a flagstone floor and was spartan. The bedroom upstairs, which I shared with two other farmhands, had the bare necessities. The bedrooms allocated to the manager and the housekeeper had rugs but fell short of being comfortable. The workers clearly were not meant to stay too long in bed.

The farm, like another in Glen Dochart, was owned by two brothers – Willieson. One, a retired army captain and a bachelor, had his lush living quarters in one end of the farmhouse. Aunt Johan cooked and cleaned for him and he was well looked after, all for twenty-four pounds a term! (six months). Fresh grilled trout was one of his favourite suppers and I was privileged, unknown to him, to savour the flavour of fresh Tay trout!

The farmhouse had a commanding view some seven miles up the glen from Killin. During my few months on the farm, I was able to cycle round parts of Tayside and relate the majesty of the surrounding bens, lochs and rivers to Sir Walter Scott's *Lady of the Lake*, portions of which were still fresh in my memory. The Trossachs and Loch Achray were not so very far away.

Some pressure was applied to turn me into a shepherd but I was having none of it. The one and only time during the first week of my arrival that I 'took to the hill' with other shepherds, was an unhappy experience for me. The mist came swirling down some miles up the glen and, being of a tender age, I was told to stay put in a small cave until the rest of the shepherds returned. I knew better than to wander in the mist, as I would only go in circles if no misadventure were to befall me! I was damp and miserable and as the morning turned to noon – at least I thought it was noon, but I had no luxury such as a watch – the effects of the morning's porridge gave way to pangs of hunger and my thoughts were of my home in Raasay. Homesickness and self-pity gave way to tears. I took stock of myself, turned off the tear taps and resolved there and then that sheep care was not for me. The mist cleared up in its own effortless way and

182

the shepherds were back with plenty of dogs but no sign of any sheep. Murdo the manager took stock of the situation – if not of the sheep on that occasion – and after some remonstration on my part, I was from then on given the job of milking seven cows by hand, twice daily, feeding the stirks, keeping the farm steading, including the byre, clean and helping Aunt Johan with the food for some ten hungry shepherds, two of whom – the Macarthur brothers – came from as far away as Glen Lyon.

My pay was set at three pounds per calendar month. The owner made the point that he was only obliged to settle pay at the end of term but Aunt Johan had spoken and I would receive it monthly! I wrote Aunt Mary a nice letter and enclosed two pounds out of my first pay packet, all for herself. She was thrilled.

It was not unusual when the shepherds were on the farm for their evening meal to start with a plate of thick coarse oatmeal porridge, followed with Scotch broth and then some meat dish such as mince and tatties. I have even seen a shepherd mix his mince into his porridge! The lot was polished off with plenty of tea, scones and cheese. Though food rationing was in force, farm workers were allowed extras and I do not recall any shortages at Kenknock Farm. Perhaps Aunt Johan had a winning way with her! I was always in for special treats when Hamilton the grocer and MacNally the butcher made their weekly deliveries from Killin.

Aunt Johan, whose roots were in Raasay, insisted on grace and the return of thanks being said at mealtimes but private or family worship was held at bedtime only. The local minister called one afternoon. She being a kindly soul and a Highlander, insisted that he stay for tea. She provided the usual good spread of home baking. There was no visible sign that he had asked for a blessing. It was evident that he had finished his tea when he stood up and handed her a tract –

but there was still no acknowledgement to the Most High.

'Will you return thanks before I take away the teatray,' said the intrepid Johan.

'Well, Mrs Macleod, thank you very much for the tea. I will call again if I am spared.'

'Well, well – if you are dead I shall not expect you,' was the quick rejoinder. Regaining her composure after his departure, she was heard to mutter, 'What can you expect – he belongs to the Church of Scotland.'

I did not care for the nature of the work on the farm, other than the catering part. I suppose that, though on a larger scale, I saw the various duties in my subconscious as being not dissimilar to those on the croft – a way of life not much to my liking. The neighbouring farmers and farm-hands were considerate and kind. I was made to feel like an immediate member of the family and the evening interlude was always pleasant. Aunt Johan, who by nature was jolly, enjoyed a game of cards and we joined in the fun. There was of course no gambling. I knew from our private chats over cups of tea when we had the house to ourselves, that she worried deeply for the safety of two of her sons, by then in the Royal Air Force, but she hid her concern remarkably well and was pleasant to everyone.

I was pleasantly surprised to find that card playing was acceptable. Although as a lad in Torran we were permitted games such as 'Ludo' and 'Snakes and Ladders', cards were not allowed. They were associated with Satan. Someone, who should have known better, once sent a pack of cards to his young cousin in Arnish, only to have them burnt, together with the 'contaminated' wrapping paper and string, by the old dear of church flowers fame.

The farm was sold at the November term and for me it was a neat way out. On a frosty morning in late November, I was off to join, in Mallaig, one of David MacBrayne's steamers, the *Loch Mor*, as a cabin boy – a berth secured for

184

me by Cousin Iain, a brother of the farm manager and second steward on the vessel.

Although it was deep into winter, Mallaig seemed to have more appeal than when I passed through in summer. The day was calm and the weather was warmer than in the Perthshire glens. I was welcomed on board by Captain Robertson, known affectionately, I found out years later, as 'Squeaky Robertson'! Indeed, many years later I got to know one of his sons, Norman, through our mutual involvements in the Gaelic Society of London.

The living quarters in the *Loch Mor* were comfortable. The pantry gleamed and there was little ship movement whilst alongside in Mallaig. Shortly after sailing the situation as far as I was concerned took a dramatic turn. Down below became squeamishly warm as the ship heaved, rocked and rolled on the way to Lochmaddy – or was it Castlebay? The aroma from the galley was overpowering and a glimpse of fat roast pork going down the cook's gullet was just too much for an upset stomach. I was very seasick and quite unable to do any work. My distress was met with a mixed reception from the second steward (cousin Iain); the additional workload would after all fall on him.

The *Loch Mor* left Mallaig on Monday afternoon and arrived by way of the Outer Isles at Kyle of Lochalsh on Tuesday evening. I could see Duncaan in the passing and the temptation was too much. I was off at Kyle, much to the second steward's dismay, but I was beyond the stage where an apology was appropriate. I had not signed a shipping agreement (Home Trade Articles) so fortunately the parting was amicable. Next evening I boarded the *Loch Ness* which, during the war, called on alternate days at Raasay, on the way to Stornoway. The wind was blowing from the southwest and Raasay Pier was vulnerable. I was in terror that the steamer would pass by leaving me to be tossed about the Minch for a further two days! The Master, Captain

Macarthur, knew his ship and did his stuff – I was back home on terra firma with my marine experience fading quickly from my mind, like a bad dream.

Raasay was a hive of activity. The demolition of the iron ore works was in full swing. Before and during the First World War there was a concentration of effort to extract the ore, but here we were seeing a complete turn-about, with everything under the hammer in the midst of another world war. Who can fathom the workings of the minds of industrialists! Two sawmills were working overtime at Millpark and the tree plantation was truly under the axe. Between wood and scrap metal there could be no doubt about Raasay's material contribution to the war effort. The naked hillsides were bleak and uninviting and all these activities in woodland did nothing for the ecology.

Within days, with the help of cousin Morag in Kyleakin (there was no shortage of obliging cousins), I was ensconced in the King's Arms Hotel as 'Boots'. My pay, all found, was one pound weekly, paid fortnightly. In modern day terms of percentages, my wages status had improved by some 44 per cent. It was a long day for the hotel staff from seven o'clock in the morning to eleven o'clock at night. Overtime payments had not yet been invented – not in hotels anyway – but long hours of work did not worry us and it crossed no-one's mind that the world might owe us a living. At least we had not been sold at a hiring fair and knew nothing about Fred Kitchen's Diary!

Breakfast on weekdays was porridge, followed by tea and as much toast as one cared to make. There was a good lunch and 'high tea' in the evening with no restrictions on cups of tea in between, other than that the users had to wash up their own cups. On Sunday, we enjoyed bacon and eggs for breakfast, also a very good lunch, but the evening meal was restricted to unlimited tea and toast and a limited amount of cheese, the purchase of which was in any case subject to

186

ration coupons. Mr Weir (the proprietor) and his family ate exactly the same food as the staff.

My job, apart from polishing boots and shoes, completed by chalking the room number on the soles, included the disposal each morning of numerous scuttles of coal ash (the cinders had to be retained for fuel). I disgorged the ash and other refuse on to the pebbly beach immediately below the hotel. I cannot think that the practice would be permitted these days – but hydro electricity probably makes the point an academic one. The hotel, at that time, generated its own electricity. The plant was forever giving trouble and the expertise of ships' engineers on shore leave – in the hotel bar naturally – came in useful from time to time. One engineer found his way into the kitchen and within weeks had married Mary the cook, a hefty lass from Ardroag, who knew her onions. We said goodbye to good pastry as well as to Mary and, like the guests, had to put up with 'Hobson's choice' of sago for pudding with monotonous regularity until the arrival of another good cook, Katie from Roag, who soon disposed of the sago stock by including it as an ingredient in steamed fruit pudding which from then on was regarded as a speciality of the hotel and much in demand.

My hotel duties also included a considerable amount of bar work, including the serving of drinks to the public. Beer was drawn off a barrel by natural draught, with a gantry which held five barrels. Each barrel held eighteen gallons of Deuchar's best. Strictly speaking, the correct description for a wooden cask of eighteen gallons' capacity is a half barrel. The continuous stooping to meet 'shipping orders' was bad enough, but procuring the beer on occasions was worse. The consignment, due to wartime restrictions, was sometimes no more than eight barrels. Once it arrived at the Kyleakin Ferry slipway, it was not considered economical to use a lorry for delivery to the hotel, about a quarter of a mile

187

away. I had to trundle the beer and 'roll out the barrel' a good part of the way. The beer took hours to settle – I took a little less time to cool off. The 'degree of perception in advance of his years' as recorded in the reference from my school teacher in Torran may have rubbed off on my physique – but I was still only over sixteen! Anyway, the hotel proprietor was a Justice of the Peace, the nearest policeman in Skye was based in Broadford and there was a war on.

The fleet based in the Kyles of Lochalsh was ample evidence that we were not in the tourist season. The 'season' other than when the fleet put out to sea for a few days, on minelaying operations, became a way of life. The allocated quota of spirits permitted for sales distribution as well as gallons of Deuchar's ale were consumed by thirsty sailors, and not a little by many of the locals who had their own out-of-hours 'licensing' arrangements in the taproom adjacent to Monty the tailor's shop.

The facilities afforded by Monty dried up when he joined the army, but life was not too uncomfortable in 'Number One' – the room set aside by a considerate hotel keeper for the use of the coach and mail drivers who covered scattered areas of Skye such as Sleat, Elgol and Portree, and were obliged to wait many hours in Kyleakin for the oft delayed arrival of passengers and mail in a government protected area.

The minelayers, *Southern Prince*, *Agamemnon*, *Menestheus*, *Port Quebec* and *Port Napier*, originally merchant ships of the Prince, Blue Funnel and Port Lines, were 'commandeered' and the crews, as I learnt later on, were identified as 'T124X'. Support ships included a number of American 'Lease-Lend' destroyers – names such as *Lancaster* and *St Mary* come to mind – and heavier very fast craft. *Venture*, *Manxman* and *Welshman* also were regulars in the Kyles at that stage of the war.

The *Port Napier* caught fire shortly before I went to Kyleakin. Quick action prevented a massive explosion and there was no loss of life as far as is known, but she was a total loss and the hulk may be seen to this day at low water mark in an inlet of the Kyles behind Kyleakin, known as Loch na Beist (the Loch of the Beast).

The Lochalsh Hotel was the nerve centre of naval operations and in close proximity was a base for WRNS, known locally as 'the Wrennery'. There was plenty of social life on both sides of the Kyles and a spate of weddings. Some couples settled in the area after the war, established themselves in business and brought up families. The era of the 'white settlers' came later.

During my time in Kyleakin my father had remarried and, although the family were sympathetic, our previous home life was to some extent affected. Aunt Mary was getting on in years and my young sister, barely out of school, was left to cope as best she could. Any financial support that I could give was always a help. My hotel duties had been extended and a bit more money came my way through a wage increase of ten shillings weekly and an ex gratia payment of one pound fortnightly which was always handed to me with – but separately from – the pay envelope just in case I should assume too much!

Work in the hotel had broadened my outlook and certainly my job experience. I had seen seafarers in low spirits and in high spirits. On the whole, they were well behaved and respected an island way of life. The call of the sea must have been in my blood and I suppose it was natural that with so much shipping and ships' talk around, my thoughts should turn to the sea once more.

Danish seamen who had fled their country in fishing boats, after the invasion of Denmark, were regular bar visitors. Their boats were used by the navy and I was on the point of taking up a berth on one called *Vogel*, when the local shipping agent, who I surmised took me for a lad from Harris, offered me a berth in an oil tanker, based at that time off Balmacara in the Kyles of Lochalsh, and flying the Blue Ensign. I accepted, and it was the start of a lifetime's career. In some pocket of my mind were thoughts of Catriona, a fair haired lass from Skye who had been on the staff of the King's Arms Hotel and had left to join the services some months previously.

CHAPTER 7

SEA BREEZES

On a fine summer morning, having said my goodbyes to old Mr Weir, whose standard greeting and farewell was always 'aye aye' – and the many friends I had made in the hotel, I stepped aboard the *Cuillin* and was speedily ferried across the Kyles. In those days, approaching from Skye, Kyle presented a slippery slipway leading to the 'norwest' and beyond, with the shipping agent's office perched crazily on a crag overlooking the railway station for which Ben na Cailleach at least provided scenic relief. Stepping ashore at Kyle on this July morning was for me a passport to a new life whose sorrows and joys I was to share over the next four decades.

Having successfully, if slowly, descended a perpendicular ladder which for some reason seemed to jut out ominously much further at the top, I found myself rockingly established on a narrow ledge of a liberty boat. After further descent without mishap past a varied assortment of humanity with a 'night before' or 'morning after' look, we were on our way. After numerous calls on ships in the harbour, we were alongside a tanker – drab, grey and massive. 'All on board for the "Dip",' roared someone above the chuff of the engine. I took my turn and scrambled up what I soon learnt was known as a Jacob's ladder and found myself on a dreary-looking deck littered with pipelines and valves as if thrown about at random at some builder's whim who cared not a row of pins for symmetry.

191

Duncan, who I soon learnt came from Staffin and knew all about diatomite, was all set to become a deckhand and it was his job as an assistant steward that I was taking on. He now took over and steered me through a doorway where I had to step high because of what is known as a storm step. I followed him down a very clean stairway ever afterwards to be called a companionway and then into the sleeping quarters – the 'gloryhole'.

'There's your bunk,' he said. 'It is really comfortable with a shelf beside you but mind your head and don't forget to look when you are getting up.' I was top tier. 'There's your locker – wardrobes are for home – and everyone takes turns to make tea or cocoa at night, except the chief cook.'

There were six bunks in this space above the waterline on the port side aft. Six lockers, a settle, second cook's radio, Alastair's books and Geordie's chanter, completed the furniture. As I fitted the last silver crested button in my white jacket I was greeted by Alastair, the second steward. He and I were to work together and as time went on I found him to be one of the best natured and sincerest of young men. He was not cut out to be a steward but that is another story. Later in life he was ordained as a minister of the Free Church of Scotland.

'My name is Alastair. I am sure we will get along fine. Do you play football?' (The ship was big, but where I wondered could we play football? A game of football was the last thing I wanted to think about.)

Like cousin Alick in my schooldays, my braces had given way and I had no belt. 'Ach don't worry – here is an old tie that I never wear.' Needs must and Alastair saved my immediate problem. Whoever thought of belts deserved a medal.

'Come along with me now and I'll show you the saloon and you can also meet the others.'

'Never mind the others,' I said, 'I'm ready for breakfast.'

Alastair grinned. 'You do not have breakfast until the Old

Man (Captain) is served, and watch the old fellow. He is a real fusspot. There is something wrong with his head. He had an accident during an air raid on Liverpool and his head keeps swelling ever since. We call him "Bigger Lugs" – and you can guess how it is pronounced.'

'Well, isn't he entitled to a big head if he wants one?'

'Oh, don't say things like that, John – always remember you are entitled to absolutely nothing on a ship and do help me at boat drill as I am hopeless at tying knots.'

I was seeing ship life from a new angle – boat drill, big head, no entitlements and breakfast sometime!

'Here is the saloon. The Agent will be with us for breakfast and he always sits beside the captain. The chief engineer is next in seniority to the captain. He has very little to say but he likes crisp bacon and fat beef well done. He is a Geordie.'

I had no idea what a 'Geordie' was but thought it best to say nothing and find out later.

'Now have we got everything on the table? Sugar, milk, butter, *bainne*.' At least, he does know some Gaelic, I thought, but I was soon to learn that Alastair went through this performance every mealtime and I never found out if he knew that milk and *bainne* were the same thing. Not that it was very like milk really – it was as blue as my Aunt's Etzell water.

We stepped into the pantry. George from Barleyport was trimming toast. The teapot was brimming over from the geyser and some cockroaches were active on the bulkhead above the rosy bucket. I placed my hand against the hotpress and promptly had a shock. 'Never do that,' said George. 'There is a short circuit or something.' I did not like this pantry with its silly contraptions and George exuding efficiency from all angles into its many nooks and crannies.

'Would you like some tea?'

'Yes, indeed, thank you.'

193

He gave me a funny look. 'You'll soon learn not to be so polite. Have a cup and be quick. Watch the chief steward does not see you as we are not supposed to have any just now.'

I did as I was told, but on reflection, I suspected that George, who had hoped to get my job, would have been quite happy had I been caught out! Hardly had I finished when the chief steward appeared. I had met him previously when on one of his many boozing sprees in Kyleakin. Recognition was instant and the look in his eyes suggested that it was he who might be on the defensive. He was an affable fellow and by all accounts knew his job but his main interests in life seemed to be a 'Wren' and yeast brew. He loved Deuchar's and was also partial to Scotch. Our encounter over, I ran into George merrily clanging a bell. It was the signal for breakfast.

I took up my station at the table which accommodated all the junior officers and coped quite well. The Old Man (Captain Anderson), who was always punctual, was by now in his place with Alistair hovering over him. The agent, first mate, second mate, chief engineer, second engineer, third engineer and the radio operator ('Sparks'), were duly seated and completed the company. All ate porridge – other breakfast cereals were not permitted. Sausages and bacon, complemented by fried bread, followed. The 'Old Man', true to form, had to be different and he insisted on one small sausage only, with mustard. Alastair produced this wizened piece of butcher's mystery and as it rolled and rollicked from side to side of a very large plate, placed plate complete with sausage reverently in front of the Master, who gave it one long look and for some reason known only to himself, burst out laughing!

After breakfast, the saloon tables were cleared completely and the whole ship's company was summoned to 'sign on'. There were no telephones or other modern communication

194

methods linking up aft, midships and the fo'c's'le (forecastle). Messengers were dispatched from the ship's bridge and no time was lost. The engineers and caterers lived aft. The deck officers were midships with some ten army and navy personnel (DEMS – Defensibly Equipped Merchant Ships) housed on the welldeck and the petty officers, deckhands and firemen were all housed in the forecastle, by the ship's bow. Some crewmen said that the rattle of the anchor chains lulled them to sleep. Donald John, who had once been a shepherd in the Falkland Islands, still counted sheep, so said Ruaridh 'Beans' from Dunevegan. Alick Campbell, also from Dunvegan, and one of the firemen-greasers, said it was a matter of attitude, age and the opportunity to have a dram or two or three.

Signing-on meant appending signatures to two registers indicating acceptance of the Articles of Agreement. This formidable document entitled us among other things, subject to substitution, to a quarter of an ounce of pepper each week and a pound of bread daily, provided the ship's cook was in good health and there was good weather. It was not clear how these provisos were to be defined, especially the former, as no doctor was carried. With everything as clear to me as mud or the sheep's dipping trough at Glam, I moved towards the table. The captain glowered at me, told me to speak up and without further ado I heard myself being christened 'Whispering Grass', a nickname which I am glad to record did not catch on. He was a funny fellow who seemed to possess the knack of making his ears protrude further than ever when in a temper. He was often in a temper, which in turn gave way to minor heart attacks, confirmed by the ever decreasing digitalis tablets in the ship's medicine chest. Still, his bark was worse than his bite, as many of the crew could testify. He fed the Balmacara seagulls every afternoon and was naturally very popular with them.

He certainly was not popular with Alastair who had to make the toast daily on the Old Man's standing orders and serve it at three o'clock precisely with tea, on a silver tea-tray service. The toast was never eaten and this daily performance revealed yet another twist in the outlook on life by this 'manager of men'. Buttered toast for seagulls, even if he did believe in reincarnation and claimed to identify a former shipmate whom he last saw between two waves off Cape Horn, at a time when people ashore enjoyed less than an ounce of butter for each person weekly gave me personally some food for thought.

Herring in tomato sauce featured on the menu one evening. Alastair, as usual, served him. 'Yes, I'll have herring – without the tomato sauce.'

'Very good sir.'

The chief cook, who came from Falkirk and had previously been a fireman, was on pantry service (the chief steward was on a bender) and did not like the 'Old Man'; he was quick to refuse the request on the grounds that as the herring was canned it was not practical to serve it free of sauce. Alastair grinning broadly, passed on the message.

'I know the herring is in the sauce – get that —— grin off your face and serve me my herring without the tomato sauce.'

I had heard expletives before but this was briny stuff indeed. Watching the proceedings with the help of the saloon mirror, I saw the cook change colour and at great speed he helped Alastair to remove under the cold water tap the last particle of vegetable or fruit that adorned the pride of Lochfyne. With whispered 'blessings' it was dispatched to the table to a man who, like a spoilt brat, always got exactly what he wanted.

The chief cook himself needed no lessons in autocracy. He was immaculately clean about his person and that is about all that could be said in his favour. Were it not for the good personality and standards displayed by Duncan, the second cook, discontent would have been rife. Duncan, in later years, rose to high rank in a Clyde-based major shipping organisation. The chief cook was a firm follower of the 'Board of Trade' food scales for Merchant Seamen and he had his own measurements for 'pound and pint' issues. Even the soup was measured and I recall that he used a galvanised bucket for that purpose! (no-one talked of pails) – and the two enamel ones on board were for the exclusive use of the Master and the chief engineer for the dhobying (washing).

Soups were usually vegetable or split pea, but they were made on board and were good. Ordinary Seaman Norman Shaw, who came from Harris and joined the police after the war, got on the wrong side of the cook for allegedly pinching a packet of table salt from the galley. In those days such refinements as table salt were not for the crew tables! Donald, also from Harris (Mollinginish) and nicknamed 'Peegro', helped me keep the engineer's quarters clean. He used enough carbolocene to scrub out Chatham Barracks twice daily but he was great fun.

John-Alick, my fellow islander, always beat us to it hoisting the flag for the mailboat. He possessed a unique flair for the preparation of salads and was a good shipmate, joining in many of our 'gloryhole' discussions which incidentally ranged over many themes, but religion or politics were taboo. This cheerful young man who later on escaped the hazards of war in the western seas, died in October 1946 at sea on the *Cape Douglas*. There is a fraternal bond between seafarers, and in our case, there was a strong island one also. Memories dim in the mists of time but one does not forget.

The firemen were forever pinching teacakes (*tabnabs*) through the porthole of the engineer's pantry. They enjoyed little enough by way of such luxuries. Donald and I, with some help from Duncan, the second cook, kept forgetting to close the porthole. The chief cook was branded a 'company's man', which carried the stigma of being mean with the food. He was also called other names, usually out of his hearing if only to avert tummy troubles. In the crew's book, the cook had plenty of pepper, prunes and power. He was not to be trusted but considerations for the 'inner man' were paramount and 'least said, soonest mended' was their motto, except when food quantity and variety were no longer the spice of life. On occasions, food complaints landed on the Master's 'plate'. For a few days afterwards; cook and crew played a 'cat and mouse' game. The second cook did his best to mediate but the cook threw rank, and any improvement in the crew's cuisine was shortlived. I thought the variation in standards of community care for levels of rank on board was inexcusable and not justified. My previous catering experience, limited as it was, had started to register and helped to set me on course in my career.

The crew had mashed potatoes for breakfast without fail, accompanied with choice food such as unchined 'lamb' chops and ox liver. The amount of jacket potatoes (boiled) that found their way to the crew messrooms at lunchtime was phenomenal – all the doing of the Scalpay lads, so said Ferguson, a deckhand from Glasgow of Highland stock. The crew were not given chicken and when on Sunday, with monotonous regularity, the officers were eating fowl, the crew's bill of fare was pork. It made no sense either from the point of view of cost control or food variety and indicted both shore and ship management. These days are long gone and the modern seafarer can have birds for the picking (of a different kind) and still enjoy the company of Miss Piggy.

Donald and I had eight engineers to look after between us. We were given a morning call (put on the shake) by a crew watchman at five-thirty and were on duty by six o'clock. The first job was to give tea to the engineers on watch. There were acres of alleyways to clean down below –

and Donald did not spare the carbolocene! The cabins had wash-hand basins but no running water. It was our job to provide each cabin with a bucket of cold water and a can of boiling water every morning. The used water gurgled into an oblong container (compactum) which fitted in below the hand basin. It too had to be emptied daily and kept scrupulously clean. Ships' engineers were not the most tidy of the human breed but in my experience they were appreciative of the service provided. Their own job in the bowels of the engine-room called for training, hard work and dedication. I would have hated working a four-hour shift, twice within every twenty-four hours, in a hot and stuffy ship's engine-room with fumes and the smell of oil around me. The engineers on board this, my first deep-sea ship, which incidentally was called *Empire Diplomat*, were a considerate bunch. Donald and I did not spurn the greenbacks that came our way at the end of the voyage.

The second engineer's cabin was always in a mess no matter how much it was tidied up. One day I dumped an assortment of nuts and bolts that I found on a shelf under the compactum. It was as if the rivets had fallen out of the bottom of the engine-room. The chief engineer breathed blue breath for days. The mate's assurance that nothing was really lost if you knew where it was, afforded him no comfort. I contented myself by keeping out of the way, but all the engineers' cabins were devoid of engine-room stock thereafter.

Meal-times made their own demands. The first breakfast started at twenty past seven (seven bells). Meals had to suit the watchkeepers and the day workers. The last meal finished at six o'clock, other than what was known as a 'blackpan' for the fireman-greaser on the 'four to eight' watch. He had the benefit of the left-overs! There was no cooking overnight. Night hunger had to be satisfied with sandwiches, which for us was an afternoon chore. Some were eaten, usually by young engineers. Others, like the 'Old Man's' toast, fed the fishes and the seagulls. It was not the done thing to consult the consumer about sandwich fillings. It was corned beef, cheese or jam – end of story.

The cleaning of brass, of which there was an inordinate amount, took up hours of our time. Portholes, water boilers, electric lamp holders, door foot plates and door knobs were gleaming. How I wished that the Arnish woman of flower seeds and brass knobs fame could have seen our handiwork!

Brass cleaning was not productive labour. The brass looked pretty but the work was never-ending. Still, labour was cheap. The recognition of fixed hours of work and in consequence, the introduction of overtime payments, soon changed the scene in the immediate post-war years. Labour could not be spared for such niceties and brass gave way to other metals and plastics.

Bed-linen and towels were changed weekly for the officers. Sheets and towels were not provided for crew use and crew members were expected to wash the one and only pillow case supplied against a signature, when they joined the ship. We in the gloryhole had sheets and towels, but only because we acquired them by a sleight of hand arrangement when dealing with the weekly change of linen for the officers, who incidentally were supplied with three towels on each occasion. The weekly linen change was effected without fail every Sunday morning, after breakfast. The arrangement was a merchant navy tradition. I can claim the credit for having it scuppered in a large slice of shipping after I took up a shore posting – on humanitarian grounds, taking the weekly workload for sea staff into account. I do believe that there should be minimal work at least one day in seven and a Sabbatarian influence may well be a factor that has contributed to that view. It can be no more than a factor in a chain which in my own case linked industrial, personnel and management relations.

Big Murdo from Raasay, born and brought up in Arnish, with a brother and many sisters and surrounded by numerous knick-knacks, was a fireman-greaser in the ship. On return from leave, he brought a rifle on board. He told the Master, to whom the matter had been reported quickly, that he had no malicious designs on the human race and simply wanted to shoot cormorants as he had often done at home. The old fellow, much to everyone's surprise, if not alarm, acquiesced. He certainly would not have granted permission to requests of much less moment. Murdo was a good shot and he soon presented the 'Old Man' with a scart. He was shocked into acceptance and quite horrified that he was expected to eat it! He suggested giving it to the shipping agent, knowing that this gentleman was known locally as 'Scart'. This presentation did not come to pass and like the frozen chicken of a later era, in the words of Dai Jones from Swansea (where else?), it vanished 'mysteriously' and we had curried meat of a mysterious nature for many days.

Whilst Murdo was on leave in Raasay, some papers relating to a minister's wedding were entrusted to him. He lost them in circumstances unknown. After much ado, the papers were replaced, wedding notices appeared in good time and the reverend gentleman was wed in Kyle. Murdo made sure that he had time off so that he could be ashore in Kyle on the day of the wedding. With all his past tensions by then overcome, he spied the happy couple board the train – their first stage on honeymoon. There was no time to lose; he lifted his rifle and fired into space as the train gathered speed out of the station!

Pandemonium broke loose. Firing a rifle in a 'protected area', with mines stockpiled at Earbusaig nearby – Murdo was in trouble. He was seized by naval police and it took all the shipping agent's charm to satisfy a very senior officer of the Senior Service that letting off firearms was a traditional practice at Highland weddings. Murdo was handed over to the local police sergeant, a kindly man from Braes and with a soft spot for Raasay. Murdo got a wigging but within the hour he was free. An incident such as this was not to mar his day and he quaffed the usual draughts of Deuchar and the companionable nips of the *creutair* until a late hour. With his rifle by his shoulder, we were a subdued lot boarding the ship that night and the liberty boat left the ship's side at speed.

All seemed well and we took to our bunks, Alasdair by now seeing the lighter side of an incident in the Church of Scotland canteen where he and I had supper that evening. Our food helpings, which were always generous, were on this occasion even more so, and I remarked that if the good ladies gave out many more such helpings all the profits would soon be eaten. Alasdair, who must have had his mind on higher things, was shocked to think that I was referring to ancient ecclesiastics. 'Lights out,' bawled Duncan, our second cook, from Applecross or beyond. As the most senior rating, he was accepted as being in charge, and so with Geordie's chanter for a lullaby, we soon fell victim to Morpheus.

During the early hours I was awakened by some horrible wailing from the direction of the engine-room, across the alleyway outside our accommodation. I got up and on opening a door that led into the engine-room from the alley-way, I was amazed to see the engineer on watch, a Clydesider, careering up the companionway, taking two if not three steps at a time, and white as whitewash. Imagine my surprise when on pursuing the vocal cords that now filled the engine-room, I saw the watchkeeping fireman, complete with rifle, parading up and down by the door of the stokehold, regaling all who might or might not choose to listen, with his own version of an old Gaelic love-song – translated, 'Will you come with me young maiden?' ('An téid thu leam a rìbhinn òg?'). The singing was awful –

nothing to compare to the bridegroom's rendition at the wedding feast in Torran not so many years ago!

The engineer had, by the time I had collected my thoughts, disappeared into the bowels of the ship elsewhere to fortify himself with a cup of cocoa and no doubt wondering what to do next. The second engineer was a grumpy fellow who often suffered from indigestion and he did not fancy waking him up. The situation was most odd and not unnaturally nerve-wracking for a young engineer newly recruited from a fitter's yard in Fairfield, and without the slightest knowledge of the language, far less the ways of the Gael. Murdo was not of course typical of the average islander. He could not be taken seriously at the best of times and on this occasion he was simply reliving his role as an uninvited wedding guest, recalling the traditions of old times.

The second cook now came on the scene and, made of sterner stuff than I could claim, soon calmed him down and relieved him of his rifle. After some gentle persuasion and the promise of a good tuck-in from the galley on the morrow, the engineer returned to his station, assuring us that there would be no report. We returned to the gloryhole and were soon asleep.

The days were shortening. Some passed monotonously and without incident. The arrival of a naval craft for refuelling engendered a degree of excitement. Our ship was not privileged to have duty-free supplies of cigarettes and other good things from the slop chest (ship's shop) but our crew, from the captain to the cabin boy, had cash-in-hand and no-one was looking. Louis, the pumpman – from Drinishadder, Harris (the agent's wife also came from Harris) – had a rowing boat alongside, by kind permission of the 'Old Man'. It was much in demand for trips to Balmacara on Friday evenings. All the girls did not go to 'the dancing in Kyle' and Balmacara had much to offer. Louis was a great shipmate and he made sure that no-one was left behind at the end of the evening. There was no dancing in Balmacara on Saturday nights!

The navy laid on gala days and members of our ship's complement chalked up credits in rowing competitions. Louis' boat came in useful for practice rowing runs and the 'Harris Navy' was the talk of Lochalsh. Card games were popular in the gloryhole when the day's work was done. The army and naval gunners on board joined in and truth to tell, money did land on the table! The stakes were small and I cannot think that anyone became addicted to gambling – not that I approve of gambling. There were set rules and they were observed. By ten o'clock it was cocoa time and dealings were suspended, to be resumed on another evening. Books were in generous supply and with such a floating population there was no problem with exchange.

We were at sea – heaving and pitching down the west coast with the Clyde as our destination. We were not to know this officially as the Master had 'sealed orders' which had nothing in common with a sea-cook's version of a sausage roll; but ships have ears, and the 'galley wireless' which proclaimed that the ship was Clyde bound, proved to be correct. We had a few eventful weeks on the Clyde, and marine leviathans, including the *Queen Mary* and the *Queen Elizabeth*, slinking in and out of the Clyde in their grey overcoats, were quite a sight to see.

The 'Old Man' could always be relied on to add sparkle to the day's routine. He rammed an aircraft carrier and lost part of the docking bridge. On another occasion the ship dragged anchor and a Walworth Carrier loomed over our port side aft, missing by mere feet the ship's magazine.

During the period in dock which followed, in Greenock, those of us from the Highlands and Islands looked up many relatives and friends in Glasgow. Once in Glasgow, tramcar travel was wonderful and very good value, with journeys from Central Station to Partick costing no more than an old penny! People were so friendly in Glasgow – truly a warm city!

Donald John, one-time shepherd in the Falklands, met a friendly female at a late-night coffee stall. She was so kind, and he could not resist her invitation to have hospitality at her place in Norfolk Street – not the poshest part of Glasgow. Instead of going up the stairs of a tenement, she took him down the stairs – to the dunny (basement). It was so dark, a crack on the head and Donald John saw stars. There was no money to count later. He got back on board by late morning through the good offices of Gow Harrisons, the shipping agents. He was poor and penniless but got logged just the same for being adrift. 'There but for the grace of God, went I,' said Lachie from Leverburgh, when he heard of the coffee capers in St Vincent Street. Still, he took note of the location just in case he might stop for a cup of coffee after the Sunday service, as his church was only along the street. Donald John there and then found solace in a mug of ship's coffee. Although it was a case of one mug meeting another, the hot coffee was welcome, and in the circumstances it would not lead him into temptation!

Employer and employee relationship was demonstrated in rather a unique way while in dock. The crew, who were mostly non-union men, were keen to re-sign Articles of Agreement, but had little wish to become members of the National Union of Seamen – an implied condition of employment even in those days! It all ended up with the 'Old Man' appealing to his crew on the flying bridge to join the union and sign on. Some older crew members who had heard a great deal about the wickedness of unions from the pulpit, had reservations, but they were won over, not perhaps so much by the appeal from the Master, who clearly valued his crew, despite his quirks, but by the powers of persuasion and personality of Mr Ferguson, the representative of the union. He came from Tiree, was an old sailor and had complimentary tickets for many of the city ceilidhs!

The ship was at sea once more, chugging down St George's Channel. The galley wireless could not enlighten us this time. The admiralty had done their work well and the old boy was keeping his secret. A party of 'Wrens' boarded us at Milford Haven and attached a huge balloon to our mainmast. Alastair said we were going up for sure and got so confused that he failed to recognise the joint for lunch. To be on the safe side, the menu announced pork-mutton. The second cook said that he had heard of crossing potatoes and tomatoes but that this was a new one on him; the 'Old Man' wanted mint sauce, the chief asked for apple sauce and 'Sparks' called for crackling. Alastair fled from the scene and read John Bunyan.

We were now in convoy and for some time became familiar with the route between the Clyde and the southern ports of England. Many of the crew must have the same affection for Torbay as I have. It was the favourite haven when the convoy was thought to have been spotted.

During these months at sea I had suffered spasms of seasickness but was determined not to give in. My problem was common knowledge but the malady was one I had to overcome in my own way. The 'Old Man' was sympathetic and advised me to suck barley sugar. Not only that, he made sure that some came my way. I was told later it was old lifeboat stock! I also learnt many moons later that Captain Anderson too had never got over seasickness. Perhaps that was why he said to me on one occasion that I was in good company, as Nelson was always seasick.

Towards D-Day excitement grew. We knew so little and yet so much. The ship dragged anchor once more and we were firmly embedded off the Isle of Wight – a wonderful sitting target. The crew, to a man, as far as I know, had a big 'D' stamped on their identity cards, signifying their willingness to serve with the ship on the great day. Our mail, which came care of GPO, was delivered irregularly and there was no question of leave under any circumstances; but the crew were in good heart and not discouraged even when the bang of the twelve-pounder fired by the gun crew on practice drill flattened the cook's cakes. Dan (from Harris), the oldest able seaman and the oldest person on board, had sailed before the mast. He said that he would much rather eat oatcakes anyway.

All situations have moments of humour. During one heavy air raid we were subjected to showers of shrapnel. The first mate who saw something coming dangerously near and at great speed through the skies, ducked, and in so doing hit the 'Old Man' fair and square between the eyes, with the sharp peak of his bridge cap. Funnily enough, the old fellow took it rather well and for days made a point of sporting his 'scars of war'.

It was past midnight. The pilot was on board. The glory-hole was in darkness and all were sleeping. Bang! Crash! Peegro switched the only light on in record time and we were all awake. Alarms clanged, whistles blew, the ship heeled and we, clad in life jackets and such of our clothes as we could cope with quickly, groped with unfamiliar angles and were soon on deck. The ship had struck a reef. The chief engineer, a cool Geordie if ever there was one, and Louis the Pumpman, exercising complete presence of mind, were busily turning valves on the welldeck. My thoughts turned to the first sighting I had of all these valves when I joined the ship. There is no doubt that their prompt action kept the ship afloat. It was thought at one stage that it might be necessary to abandon ship and lifeboats were at the ready. Dai Jones, the chief steward, asked Alastair and myself to help him with his four bags as he had no wish to lose his loot! Had the order to abandon ship been given, the Clydeside bosun would have seen to it that this luggage and

207

probably the person who owned it, had a wet passage.

After considerable delay – or so it seemed to us on board, who, like mushrooms, were kept in the dark – the ship docked in Newport and was fitted with cement boxes. Damage was considerable. The Admiralty no doubt were not pleased about this catastrophe, as we had been without any shadow of doubt 'booked' for the Normandy beaches. We were ordered to find our way solo to the Tyne.

On another fine summer's morning, after docking in North Shields, we congregated in the shipping office, not far from the 'Jungle' and other choice places near the Quay, and were released from our Agreements. Louis the pump-man and I stayed on for a little longer under a special Agreement (CRS3). Most of the officers and the remainder of the crew, many from Harris, some from Skye, Raasay and Applecross, left; quite a number to be caught in the strangle-hold of a ruthless sea war, in a matter of days. I have sailed with crews from all parts of the British Isles, but there was a comradeship among our own islanders that I have rarely met since.

The ship, after many visits from bowler-hatted gentlemen who usually stayed for lunch and slithered down the gangway with knowing nods, ended in the breaker's yard at Dunston on Tyne. After the war, two successive ships bore her name and the Blue Ensign gave way to the Red.

The 'Old Man', who seemed such a different person at sea from the autocrat in command of a tanker 'oiling' the fleet in the Kyles of Lochalsh not so many months ago, had to appear in London before a board of enquiry. Although the pilot takes over the navigation on boarding a vessel, the Master, in law, is still in command. He fought his case well and retained his Master's 'ticket' – to sail another day.

The Tynesiders (Geordies) had suffered severely from Germany's bombers, but the river was hustle and bustle and the riveters' hammers could be heard for many hours. The people were – and are – kindly and it was my privilege to know them. I still have fond memories of the Roman City and the Rex in Whitley Bay; Willington Quay with its plywood factory busily churning out fitments for aeroplanes; Bewick Street with its friendly post office and the rope factory where, without fail, young Tyneside apprentices were 'initiated' – and not least the home hospitality with generous helpings of 'stottie cake' and 'penaculty' at a time when rationing was tight.

Shore leave followed at the end of my assignment. My father liked nothing better than to talk and hear about ships. A refreshment together in Raasay House Hotel with a true welcome from John Ferguson and Kenny the Post, are now but memories.

It was autumn and very peaceful in Oscaig. A telegram, delivered one morning in person by 'Post Office Mary', sent me packing and on my way to another tanker in Scapa Flow.

Who do you think was the 'Old Man'?

The experiences of life from then on, both at sea and in a shore-posting dealing with seafarers, is perhaps another story. The anecdotes related may to some extent illustrate the contrasts and changes in a way of life. Thoughts of Catriona had not dimmed. Our courtship developed and marriage followed. The dictates of a demanding business life did not permit us to live in Raasay or Skye. This may well have been our loss but the clock of time cannot be put back. I would like to think that over the years we have made some contribution to our island heritage, through our work in the Gaelic Society of London and our support of kindred societies.